First World War
and Army of Occupation
War Diary
France, Belgium and Germany

25 DIVISION
74 Infantry Brigade
Royal Irish Rifles 2nd Battalion
and Worcestershire Regiment 3rd Battalion
1 November 1915 - 31 May 1918

WO95/2247/1

The Naval & Military Press Ltd
www.nmarchive.com
Published in association with The National Archives

Published by

The Naval & Military Press Ltd

Unit 10 Ridgewood Industrial Park,

Uckfield, East Sussex,

TN22 5QE England

Tel: +44 (0) 1825 749494

www.naval-military-press.com

www.nmarchive.com

This diary has been reprinted in facsimile from the original. Any imperfections are inevitably reproduced and the quality may fall short of modern type and cartographic standards.

© **Crown Copyright**
Images reproduced by permission of The National Archives, London, England, 2015.

Contents

Document type	Place/Title	Date From	Date To
Heading	WO95/2247-1		
Heading	2nd Bn Roy Irish Rifles Nov 1915-Dec 1917		
Miscellaneous	Adjutant 2nd Battn The Royal Irish Rifles.		
Miscellaneous	A Form. Messages And Signals.	06/11/1915	06/11/1915
War Diary		01/11/1915	30/11/1915
Heading	3rd Div. 2/R. Ir. Rifles. Dec Vol XII		
Map			
War Diary		01/12/1915	31/12/1915
Heading	2nd Battn. Royal Irish Rifles January 1916		
Heading	74 Bde 25th Div. 2 R. Irish Rifles. Jan Vol XIII		
War Diary		01/01/1916	31/01/1916
Heading	2nd Battn. Royal Irish Rifles. February. 1916		
War Diary		01/02/1916	29/02/1916
Heading	2nd Battn. Royal Irish Rifles. March 1916		
Miscellaneous	A. G's Office Base		
War Diary		01/03/1916	31/03/1916
Heading	2nd Battn. Royal Irish Rifles, April 1916		
War Diary	Chelers Sheet 36B 1/40,000 U.22.a	01/04/1916	07/04/1916
War Diary	Chelers (36 B) U 22 a	08/04/1916	10/04/1916
War Diary	Ternas B 9.d	11/04/1916	22/04/1916
War Diary	Trenches about S 22	23/04/1916	27/04/1916
War Diary	Camblain L'Abbe	28/04/1916	28/04/1916
War Diary	Cabaret Rouge S 13 d 78 Sheet 36 C	28/04/1916	28/04/1916
War Diary	Camblain L'Abbe W 22 Sheet 36 B	29/04/1916	30/04/1916
Heading	2nd Battn. Royal Irish Rifles. May, 1916		
Miscellaneous	Duplicate War Diaries.	03/05/1916	03/05/1916
War Diary	Camblain L'Abbe W. 22 (36b)	01/05/1916	03/05/1916
War Diary	Trenches s. 22 (36c)	04/05/1916	09/05/1916
War Diary	Zouave Valley and Cabaret Rouge	10/05/1916	13/05/1916
War Diary	S. 22 (36c)	14/05/1916	17/05/1916
War Diary	Trenches S. 22 (36c)	17/05/1916	20/05/1916
War Diary	Averdoingt	21/05/1916	31/05/1916
Miscellaneous	D.A.G. 3rd Echelon Base	15/05/1916	15/05/1916
Heading	2nd Battn. Royal Irish Rifles. June 1916		
War Diary		01/06/1916	22/06/1916
War Diary	Canaples	25/06/1916	25/06/1916
War Diary	Bonneville	26/06/1916	28/06/1916
War Diary	Mirvaux	29/06/1916	30/06/1916
Heading	2nd Battalion The Royal Irish Rifles July 1916		
War Diary	Harponville	01/07/1916	01/07/1916
War Diary	Senlis	02/07/1916	03/07/1916
War Diary	Bouzincourt	04/07/1916	06/07/1916
War Diary	La Boisselle	07/07/1916	10/07/1916
War Diary	Senlis	11/07/1916	15/07/1916
War Diary	Trenches (Ovillers)	16/07/1916	16/07/1916
War Diary	Bouzincourt	17/07/1916	18/07/1916
War Diary	Beauval	19/07/1916	21/07/1916
War Diary	Bus Les Artois	22/07/1916	24/07/1916
War Diary	Trenche	25/07/1916	29/07/1916
War Diary	Mailly Maillet Wood	30/07/1916	31/07/1916

Type	Description	From	To
Heading	2nd Battalion Royal Irish Rifles August 1916		
War Diary	Mailly Maillet Wood	01/08/1916	07/08/1916
War Diary	Trenches at 4d Central	08/08/1916	13/08/1916
War Diary	Bus Les Artois	14/08/1916	18/08/1916
War Diary	N. Bluff 57D S.E. 1/20,000 Sq 36 Central E Bank of R Ancre	19/08/1916	28/08/1916
War Diary	Map 57D SE Trenches X 33 C 70 to X 2 b 48	28/08/1916	29/08/1916
War Diary	Map 57D SE 1/20,000 Trenches X 33 C 70 to X 2 b 48	30/08/1916	31/08/1916
Heading	2nd. Royal Irish Rifles September 1916		
War Diary	Sheet 57 D 1/40,000 Sq X 3	01/09/1916	01/09/1916
War Diary	Bde Reserve	02/09/1916	03/09/1916
War Diary	Bde Reserve Sheet 57 D 1/40,000	04/09/1916	06/09/1916
War Diary	Acheux	07/09/1916	08/09/1916
War Diary	Puchevillers Map Lens II 1/10,000	08/09/1916	09/09/1916
War Diary	Beauval	10/09/1916	10/09/1916
War Diary	Berneuil	11/09/1916	12/09/1916
War Diary	Domqueur Map Lens II	13/09/1916	17/09/1916
War Diary	Map Lens II Domqueur	17/09/1916	23/09/1916
War Diary	Domqueur Map Lens II 1/100,000 Beauval	24/09/1916	25/09/1916
War Diary	Forceville	25/09/1916	25/09/1916
War Diary	Hedauville Sheet 57D SE 1/20,000	26/09/1916	27/09/1916
War Diary	Trenches Sheet 57D SE 1/20,000	28/09/1916	30/09/1916
Heading	2nd Battn. Royal Irish Rifles October 1916		
War Diary	Trenches and Engle Belmer Map Sheet 57 D 1/20,000	01/10/1916	01/10/1916
War Diary	Englebelmer	02/10/1916	02/10/1916
War Diary	Camp W 8 Central	03/10/1916	04/10/1916
War Diary	Camp W 8 Central Map Sheet 57D SE	05/10/1916	05/10/1916
War Diary	Ovillers Post	06/10/1916	06/10/1916
War Diary	In Reserve	07/10/1916	07/10/1916
War Diary	In Reserve B.H.Q. R 28d 14	08/10/1916	13/10/1916
War Diary	Trenches	14/10/1916	15/10/1916
War Diary	Map Refenuel Sheet 57 D SE Trenches Abert R 22 C9d	16/10/1916	23/10/1916
War Diary	H.Q. in Sheet No 67a	24/10/1916	24/10/1916
War Diary	Beauval	25/10/1916	30/10/1916
War Diary	Bn HQ at Q. 35 b 44 (Map Ref B Serices 27 D S.E.)	31/10/1916	31/10/1916
Heading	2nd Battn. Royal Irish Rifles. November 1916		
War Diary	Thieushouk (Near Caestre)	01/11/1916	01/11/1916
War Diary	Shaexhen	02/11/1916	02/11/1916
War Diary	Bn HQ. at	04/11/1916	04/11/1916
War Diary	Bn HQ at U.21.a.3.7 Map Ref. St Yves 1:10000	05/11/1916	13/11/1916
War Diary	Hope House (U.14.d.8.1) Pennanent Bn HQ ,	14/11/1916	30/11/1916
Heading	2nd Battn. Royal Irish Rifles, December 1916		
War Diary	Hope House (U14d 8.1) Bn Hd St.	01/12/1916	14/12/1916
War Diary	Regina Camp	15/12/1916	21/12/1916
War Diary	Nieppe	22/12/1916	31/12/1916
Operation(al) Order(s)	74th Infantry Brigade Operation Order No. 97	02/12/1916	02/12/1916
Miscellaneous			
Operation(al) Order(s)	74th Infantry Brigade Operation Order No. 98	19/12/1916	19/12/1916
Operation(al) Order(s)	74th Infantry Brigade Operation Order No. 99	22/12/1916	22/12/1916
Operation(al) Order(s)	74th Infantry Brigade Operation Order No. 100	27/12/1916	27/12/1916
Miscellaneous	Correction to 7th Infantry Brigade Operation Order No. 100	29/12/1916	29/12/1916
Operation(al) Order(s)	74th Infantry Brigade Order No. 102	30/12/1916	30/12/1916
War Diary	Nieppe	01/01/1917	14/01/1917
War Diary	Regina Camp	15/01/1917	17/01/1917
War Diary	Hope House	18/01/1917	29/01/1917

Type	Description	From	To
War Diary	Regina	30/01/1917	31/01/1917
War Diary	Regina Camp	01/02/1917	01/02/1917
War Diary	Romarin	02/02/1917	28/02/1917
War Diary	Tatinghem	01/03/1917	19/03/1917
War Diary	Tatinghem to Staple	20/03/1917	20/03/1917
War Diary	Staple & Strazeele	21/03/1917	22/03/1917
War Diary	To Nieppe	23/03/1917	27/03/1917
War Diary	To Oosthove Farm	28/03/1917	31/03/1917
War Diary	Oosthove Farm	01/04/1917	02/04/1917
War Diary	Ref Map Sheet 36 NW	03/04/1917	05/04/1917
War Diary	Noote Boom Ref Map Haze Brouck 5a	06/04/1917	13/04/1917
War Diary	Ref Sheet 28 SW Trench Map	14/04/1917	18/04/1917
War Diary	St Quentin Cabaret Aldershot Camp	19/04/1917	29/04/1917
War Diary	Noote Boom Ref Map Hazebrouck 5a	30/04/1917	30/04/1917
War Diary	Noote Boom (SW Bailleul)	01/05/1917	09/05/1917
War Diary	Near Eqlise	10/05/1917	18/05/1917
War Diary	Belford Camp J26A 3.9 R Map Sheet 28 S.W.	19/05/1917	21/05/1917
War Diary	Bulford Camp	22/05/1917	29/05/1917
War Diary	La Creche	30/05/1917	04/06/1917
War Diary	Bremerschen	05/06/1917	14/06/1917
War Diary	Sheet 28 T.1. 42	15/06/1917	25/06/1917
War Diary	Fruges	26/06/1917	30/06/1917
Operation(al) Order(s)	Operation Order No. 38 by Lieut-Col. H.R. Goodman, Commanding 2nd Battn. The Royal Irish Rifles.	03/06/1917	03/06/1917
War Diary	Fruges	01/07/1917	07/07/1917
War Diary	Radinghem	08/07/1917	14/07/1917
War Diary	Pioneer Camp	15/07/1917	25/07/1917
War Diary	K. 36 a 6.6	26/07/1917	26/07/1917
War Diary Map	Sheet 27 K 36a 6.6	27/07/1917	31/07/1917
Operation(al) Order(s)	Operation Order No. 59 by Major R.de. R. Rose. Comdg. 2 Bn. R. I. Rifles.	07/08/1917	07/08/1917
Miscellaneous	To all Recipients of O.O. 59	07/08/1917	07/08/1917
Miscellaneous	To all Recipients of O.O. 59		
War Diary	Swan Chateau	01/08/1917	04/08/1917
War Diary	Ramparts Ypres	05/08/1917	05/08/1917
War Diary	In the Line Bn Hd Qrs Sieben House	06/08/1917	06/08/1917
War Diary	In The Line	07/08/1917	13/08/1917
War Diary	Halifax Camp	14/08/1917	14/08/1917
War Diary	Steenvoorde	15/08/1917	17/08/1917
War Diary	Eecke	18/08/1917	19/08/1917
War Diary	J 35 d 69	20/08/1917	21/08/1917
War Diary	Steenvoorde	22/08/1917	09/09/1917
War Diary	Micmac	10/09/1917	10/09/1917
War Diary	Caestre	11/09/1917	11/09/1917
War Diary	Steenbecque	12/09/1917	12/09/1917
War Diary	Raimbert	13/09/1917	30/09/1917
Miscellaneous	Patrol Reports.		
Miscellaneous	Nominal Roll Of Officers And Other Ranks Granted Awards During Westhoek Operation		
War Diary	Raimbert	01/10/1917	04/10/1917
War Diary	Bethune	05/10/1917	05/10/1917
War Diary	In The Line	06/10/1917	12/10/1917
War Diary	Annequin	13/10/1917	18/10/1917
War Diary	In The Line	19/10/1917	24/10/1917
War Diary	Beuvry	25/10/1917	31/10/1917

Miscellaneous	List Of Officers Of "Pointer" Going Into Action		
Miscellaneous	Stores In Brigade Dump Appendix "A"		
Miscellaneous	Fighting Order Appendix "B"		
Miscellaneous	Orders For Battle Stragglers Posts. Appendix "C"		
Miscellaneous	Artillery Barrage Time Table. Appendix "C"		
Miscellaneous	Appendix "I"		
Heading	WO95/2247-2		
Heading	3rd Bn Worchester Regt Nov 1917-May 1918		
War Diary	Trenches Givenchy Festubert Sector Ref 36 SW3 S 22c 3515 to 36c NW A 3a85 55	01/11/1917	03/11/1917
War Diary	Windy Corner Ref 36 NW A 36c 80.40	04/11/1917	09/11/1917
War Diary	Annequin	10/11/1917	15/11/1917
War Diary	Trenches Cambrin Right Sub Sector Ref 36 NW G 4 a 60.100 to G 4 d 95.15	16/11/1917	23/11/1917
War Diary	Annequin	23/11/1917	25/11/1917
War Diary	Beuvry	26/11/1917	29/11/1917
War Diary	Trenches Cambrin Right Sub Sector	30/11/1917	30/11/1917
War Diary	Trenches Right Sub-Sector Cambrin	00/11/1917	00/11/1917
Miscellaneous	Casualties During November 1917		
War Diary	Cambrin Sector	01/12/1917	06/12/1917
War Diary	Ladnicourt S. Sector	07/12/1917	31/12/1917
Miscellaneous	Casualties During December 1917		
War Diary	Pronville Sector Sheet 57c 1/40000	01/01/1918	14/01/1918
War Diary	Nest D 21a 9.9 Sheet 57c	14/01/1918	31/01/1918
Miscellaneous	3rd Bn The Worcestershire Regiment	02/02/1918	02/02/1918
War Diary		01/02/1918	28/02/1918
Heading	3rd Battalion The Worcester Regiment March 1918		
War Diary	Achiet Area	01/03/1918	12/03/1918
War Diary	Map 57 C	21/03/1918	28/03/1918
War Diary	St Ouen	29/03/1918	31/03/1918
Miscellaneous	3rd Bn The Worcestershire Regiment	01/04/1919	01/04/1919
Heading	3rd Battalion The Worcestershire Regiment April 1918		
War Diary	Caestre	01/04/1918	30/04/1918
Miscellaneous	3rd Bn The Worcestershire Regt.	01/05/1918	01/05/1918
War Diary		01/05/1918	31/05/1918
Miscellaneous		25/04/1917	25/04/1917

WO95/2247/1

25TH DIVISION
74TH INFY B E

2ND BN ROY. IRISH RIFLES
NOV 1915 - NOV 1917

FROM 3 DIV. 9 BDE

(To 36 DIV. 108 Bde)

19. **PASS WORD.** Password:- "VIMY".

20. **ZERO HOUR.** Zero Day and hour will be notified later.

A C K N O W L E D G E.

[signature] LIEUT.,
ADJUTANT, 2nd BATTN. THE ROYAL IRISH RIFLES.

Copies to:-
- No. 1. 74th Infantry Brigade.
- 2. Commanding Officer.
- 3. Second-in-Command.
- 4. Signalling Officer.
- 5. Medical Officer.
- 6. O.C. "A" COMPANY.
- 7. O.C. "B" COMPANY.
- 8. O.C. "C" COMPANY.
- 9. O.C. "D" COMPANY.
- 10. O.C. 74th M.G.C.
- 11. O.C. 74th T.M.B.
- 12. O.C. 13th Cheshire Regiment.
- 13. War Diary.
- 14. File.

"A" Form.
MESSAGES AND SIGNALS.

Army Form C 2121.
(In pads of 100.)
No. of Message..............

Prefix......Code......m	Words.	Charge.	This message is on a/c of :	Recd. at ....m.
Office of Origin and Service Instructions.	Sent			Date
	At............m.		............Service.	From ....
	To............			
	By............		(Signature of "Franking Officer.")	By............

TO: ALL RECIPIENTS OF OPERATION ORDER NO 35.

Sender's Number.	Day of Month.	In reply to Number.	**A A A**
A.C 28	4/6		

Reference Operation Order No 35 AAA FOLLOWING amendments AAA Para 5 (a).T ZERO plus 50 read at ZERO plus 70 AAA before "WM" erase " " insert "OCCUR and " AAA Para 6. Total number of sandbags should read 220 AAA

From: O.C. 2nd ROYAL IRISH RIFLES.
Place:
Time:

The above may be forwarded as now corrected. (Z)

Censor. Signature of Addressor or person authorised to telegraph in his name.

LIEUT-COL.

* This line should be erased if not required.

WAR DIARY or INTELLIGENCE SUMMARY

Army Form C. 2118.

MAP REFERENCES - BELGIUM and FRANCE - SHEET 36

Hour, Date, Place	Summary of Events and Information	Remarks and references to Appendices
1915 1ST November	In trenches at LE TOUQUET. Very quiet day. Extremely hot. Casualties Nil	10,000
2ND November	In trenches as above. Battalion relieved by 13th Cheshire Regiment commencing at 4.30 pm and complete at 7.30 pm. Went into billets at LE BIZET. Quiet day. Casualties Nil	
3rd	In billets as above. GAPPA MAJOR C.B. EAMES - Connaught Rangers joined the battalion	
4th	In billets as above. 2ND LT F.K.WHITE 2nd Royal Irish Rifles and 2ND LT T.J. JENKINSON 4th R.I. Fusiliers to hospital sick	
5/11	In billets as above	
6/11	In billets as above	
7/11	In billets as above	

Army Form C. 2118.

WAR DIARY
or
INTELLIGENCE SUMMARY.
(Erase heading not required.)

Hour, Date, Place	Summary of Events and Information	Remarks and references to Appendices
1915	MAP REFERENCES – BELGIUM and FRANCE – SHEET 36 1/40,000	
November 8th	In billets at LE BIZET. 2ND LT T B FORSTER 3/Royal Irish Regiment was transferred to 2/Royal Irish Regiment. He went sick 3.10.15 and admitted into the Field Ambulance. Battalion paraded for the trenches. Companies Bombers etc leaving at short intervals. Relieved 13th Cheshire Regiment in trenches at LE TOUQUET. Relief Completed at 5.45/pm. Casualties 1. Night acts 8/9th heavy	
November 9th	Quiet In trenches as above. Quiet day. Trenches very wet- and parapets etc broken in parts. Weather more fine. Patrols went out during Night 9th/10th oct. but discovered Nothing of Much importance. Casualties Nil. 2ND LT T.S. JENKINSON rejoined from hospital JS	

WAR DIARY
or
INTELLIGENCE SUMMARY

Army Form C. 2118.

MAP REFERENCES – BELGIUM and FRANCE – SHEET 36 –

Remarks: 40,000

Hour, Date, Place	Summary of Events and Information
1915	
November 10th	In trenches as above. Very quiet day. A few rifle & M. Gun fell into trenches. Were still in a bad state. A patrol went out at night but did not discover anything of much importance. Casualties Nil.
November 11th	In trenches as above. Trenches very wet and much rain fell. Very much rifle & Enemy sent a salvo of light T.M. shells over. No damage done. Casualties Nil. Temp. Captain R. O'LONE 2nd Royal Irish Rifles KILLED while starting a listening post about 9.30 p.m. Other ranks Nil.
November 12th	In trenches as above. Night 11th/12th very quiet. Trenches very wet. Casualties Nil.
November 13th	In trenches as above. Quiet day. Trenches a little drier. Casualties Nil.

WAR DIARY
or
INTELLIGENCE SUMMARY.
(Erase heading not required.)

Army Form C. 2118.

Hour, Date, Place	Summary of Events and Information	Remarks and references to Appendices
1915	MAP REFERENCES - BELGIUM and FRANCE - SHEET 36 - 40,000	
November 14th	In trenches at LE TOUQUET. Quiet day. Trenches still wet. Battalion was relieved by 13th Cheshire Regt. Relief Complete 5.30 pm. Casualties Nil. Battalion Marched by Companies to billets in LE BIZET. 2ND LT. F.K. WHITE 2ND Royal Irish Rifles returned from hospital	
November 15th	In billets as above. Casualties Nil	
16th	In billets as above. Working party of 200 men were furnished by the Bn for cleaning etc.	
17th	In billets as above. Working party of 200 men furn. by the battalion. 9 Other ranks joined the battalion. 2ND LT. F.K. WHITE to hospital again. Casualties Nil.	
18th	In billets as above. Working party of 200 furn. by the Battalion. Casualties 3 Other ranks	

WAR DIARY
or
INTELLIGENCE SUMMARY.
(Erase heading not required.)

Army Form C. 2118.

Hour, Date, Place	Summary of Events and Information	Remarks and references to Appendices
1915	MAP REFERENCES - BELGIUM and FRANCE - SHEET 36 - 1/10,000	
November 19th	In billets at LE BIZET. The battalion was inspected by Mr JOHN REDMOND, M.P. at 3 p.m. He congratulated the battalion on its gallant conduct. The battalion then proceeded to the trenches at LE TOUQUET, marching off by Companies at ½ hour intervals, and relieved 13TH CHESHIRE RGT. Relief complete at 5.55 p.m. Casualties 1 KILLED 1 WOUNDED during relief. Captain H.R.H. IRELAND rejoined from hospital.	
20th	In trenches as above. Trenches wet, and much labour necessary to repair them. 2ND LT. T.J. THOMPSON 4/R.I. Fusiliers to hospital sick. Casualties 1 July. 2.5.m. Quiet day.	
21st	In trenches as above. Casualties Nil. Quiet day.	
22ND	In trenches as above. Quiet day. Trenches dried.	J.C.J.

WAR DIARY
or
INTELLIGENCE SUMMARY.
(Erase heading not required.)

Army Form C. 2118.

Hour, Date, Place	Summary of Events and Information	Remarks and references to Appendices
1915	MAP REFERENCES – FRANCE AND BELGIUM – SHEET 36	40,000
November 22ND	(cont) very hot, stray bullets fired June Fort. 8 other ranks joined the Battalion. Casualties 2 other ranks wounded.	
November 23rd	2 trenches as above. Patrol went out during Night. Ptes. 22nd/23rd and gained useful local information. Casualties Nil	
November 24th	In trenches as above. Quiet day. Battalion relieved by 13th Cheshire Regt. Relief somewhat delayed by enemy shelling approaches from LE BIZET. Relief complete 6 p.m. Casualties Nil	
November 25th	In billets at LE BIZET. Some frost during night. Casualties Nil.	
November 26th	In billets as above. Reinforcement of 5 other ranks joined the Battalion following officers joined the Battalion. 2ND LT. H. PHILLIPS – 5th Royal Irish Rifles 2ND LT. A.A. BROOMFIELD – 5th " " " 2ND LT. P. McMAHON – 4th " " " 2ND LT. H.W. O'REILLY – 4th " " "	

WAR DIARY
or
INTELLIGENCE SUMMARY.
(Erase heading not required.)

Army Form C. 2118.

Hour, Date, Place	Summary of Events and Information	Remarks and references to Appendices
1915	MAP REFERENCES — BELGIUM and FRANCE — SHEET 36 — 1/40,000	
November 26th	(Cont) One man actually accidentally wounded on hand throwing bombs — Casualties 1 wounded.	
November 27th	In billets at LE BIZET. Casualties Nil	
November 28th	In billets as above. Working parties furnished by Battalion. Shelled while repairing communication trenches. The M.O. proceeded at once to the place, and while attending the wounded was killed by a shell. Casualties KILLED. LT. MAURICE MACKENZIE. R.A.M.C. (attached 2nd Royal Irish Rifles). Other Ranks KILLED — 2. WOUNDED — 4.	LT W.E. BURROWS R.A.M.C. joined the battalion in place of LT. MACKENZIE.
November 29th	In billets as above. Battalion paraded by Companies and marched off by Companies at half hour intervals. First Company left LE BIZET at 5.30 p.m. This was done to avoid being shelled unduly as the road	S.C.

Army Form C. 2118.

WAR DIARY
or
INTELLIGENCE SUMMARY.
(Erase heading not required.)

Instructions regarding War Diaries and Intelligence Summaries are contained in F.S. Regs., Part II. and the Staff Manual respectively. Title pages will be prepared in manuscript.

MAP REFERENCES - BELGIUM and FRANCE - SHEET 36 - 40,000

Hour, Date, Place 1915	Summary of Events and Information	Remarks and references to Appendices
November 29th	(Cont) had been subjected to shell fire the day before somewhat severely. Relieved 13TH CHESHIRE RGT. in trenches at LE TOUQUET. Relief complete 8 pm. Casualties Nil	
30th	In trenches as above. Quiet day. Trenches in a fair condition though still very wet. No rain fell during day. About 11 am – 12 noon enemy shelled La Houssoye with 77 mm field gun. No damage done. Casualties Nil.	cqd 4/4

Superintendent Chand
Cmdg 9/R Irish Rifles
9·12·15

2/R. Ir. Rifles.
Dec
Vol XII

3rd Div
75th
28th

WAR DIARY
or
INTELLIGENCE SUMMARY.
(Erase heading not required.)

Army Form C. 2118.

Hour, Date, Place	Summary of Events and Information	Remarks and references to Appendices
19/15	MAP REFERENCES — BELGIUM and FRANCE — SHEET 36 — 1/40,000	
December 1st.	In trenches at LE TOUQUET. Quiet day. Trenches still very wet. Casualties 1 Wounded	
2nd	In trenches as above. Quiet day. Casualties Nil.	
3rd	In trenches as above. Quiet day. Casualties Nil.	
4th	In trenches as above. Quiet day. Trenches still very wet, and some rain. Casualties Nil. Battalion relieved by 13th Cheshire Regt. Relief complete 8.15 pm. Battalion proceeded to billets at LE BIZET. 2nd Lt P. ERSKINE and 2/Lt E.W.V. LEACH 3/R.I. Rifles joined.	
5th	In billets as above. Casualties Nil. Owing to the very wet state of trench GH (C10 b 5.5) it was decided to abandon that pit and build results just in rear. Accordingly "D" Coy was detailed for this work, and found continuous fatigues for this work. Casualties Nil	
6th	In billets as above. Very wet. Casualties Nil	J.C.S.

Army Form C. 2118.

WAR DIARY
or
INTELLIGENCE SUMMARY.
(Erase heading not required.)

Instructions regarding War Diaries and Intelligence Summaries are contained in F. S. Regs., Part II. and the Staff Manual respectively. Title pages will be prepared in manuscript.

Hour, Date, Place	Summary of Events and Information	Remarks and references to Appendices
	MAP REFERENCES – BELGIUM and FRANCE – SHEET – 36 – 40,000.	
December 7th	In billets at LE BIZET. Same as main. Casualties Nil	
8th 10:15	In billets as above. 2ND LIEUT A.J LE NNOX 2/R.I.Rifles (Temporary Commission) (from Cadet School) joined the battalion. 2ND LIEUT C.H. WALE 2/Royal Irish Rifles rejoined the battalion. 2ND LT PANTER - The Royal Irish Rifles joined the battalion. Casualties Nil	
9th	In billets as above. Very wet day. Relieved 13th Cheshire Regt. Relief complete 8. pm. Casualties Nil. Trenches very wet and flooded. Some trenches knee-deep over at LE TOUQUET. B. trenches as above. Quiet day, but very wet. Trenches knee deep in many places. LT. T.J.A. STEWART temporarily 3RD Royal Irish Rifles wounded. Other ranks Nil.	
10th		
11th	In trenches as above. Quiet day, a few dead of men and trenches wetter than ever.	

Army Form C. 2118.

WAR DIARY
or
INTELLIGENCE SUMMARY.
(Erase heading not required.)

Date, Hour, Place	Summary of Events and Information	Remarks and references to Appendices
	Map References — BELGIUM and FRANCE — SHEET 36.	40,000
1915 December 11th	(Cont) Lt T.S. Jenkinson 4th Royal Irish Fusiliers wounded accidentally with a Very pistol.	
12th	In trenches at LE TOUQUET. Quiet day. Trenches still very wet. 2/Lt. C.H.W. Darling 3/Royal Irish Rifles KILLED. Other ranks 2 wounded.	
13th	In trenches as above. Quiet day. Lt. Col. Swan 4/ Seaforth Rifles and Capt. Rose 1/4 Black Watch attached for instruction. Quiet day. One Other rank wounded in LE BIZET. One and other rank attached to a French Mortar Battery wounded (in another part of the line).	
14th	In trenches as above. Quiet day. Relieved by 13th Cheshire Regt. Relief complete 8.15 pm. Battalion proceeded to billets at LE BIZET. Casualties Nil.	

Army Form C. 2118.

WAR DIARY
or
INTELLIGENCE SUMMARY.
(Erase heading not required.)

Instructions regarding War Diaries and Intelligence Summaries are contained in F.S. Regs., Part II. and the Staff Manual respectively. Title pages will be prepared in manuscript.

Hour, Date, Place	Summary of Events and Information	Remarks and references to Appendices
1915	MAP REFERENCES — BELGIUM and FRANCE — SHEET-36 - 1/40,000	
December 15th	2 killed at LE BIZET. Village was slightly shelled during the day with about 15-20 shells of 77 M.M. especially in the neighbourhood of the LE BIZET Church. Casualties 1 KILLED 2 WOUNDED	
16th	2 killed as above. Draft 80 other ranks arrived.	
17th	2 killed as above.	
18th	2 killed as above.	
19th	2 killed as above. Battalion relieved 13th Cheshire Regt in trenches at LE TOUQUET. Relief complete 8.40 pm Casualties 1 Wounded	
20th	In trenches as above. Casualties Nil. Quiet day. Misty.	
21st	In trenches as above. Quiet day, except for a few half a dozen or so - 77 m.m. shells from enemy falling about 74th left of our line. Casualties Nil.	
22nd	In trenches as above. 6 other ranks joined the Bn. About 100 Enemy	

WAR DIARY
or
INTELLIGENCE SUMMARY.
(Erase heading not required.)

Army Form C. 2118.

MAP REFERENCES – BELGIUM and FRANCE – SHEET – 36 – 1/40,000.

Hour, Date, Place	Summary of Events and Information	Remarks and references to Appendices
December 22nd 1915	(Cont) 7.7 p.m. Shells fell on and around some detached posts on the left of the position occupied by the battalion. Casualties Nil.	
23rd	In trenches at LE TOUQUET. Quiet day. Casualties Nil	
24th	In trenches as above. Quiet day. The battalion was relieved by 13TH Cheshire Regt., and went into billets at LE BIZET. Casualties Nil. Relief complete 8.45 p.m.	
25th	In billets at LE BIZET. Quiet day. Casualties Nil	
26th	In billets as above. Casualties Nil	
27th	In billets as above. Casualties Nil	
28th	In billets as above. Casualties Nil	
29th	In billets as above. The battalion paraded for the trenches by Companies, and relieved 13th Cheshire Regt. in trenches at LE TOUQUET. Relief Complete 8.15 p.m. Casualties Nil.	
30th	In trenches as above. Very quiet day. Casualties Nil. 2/LIEUT. R.A. YOUNG - 4/Royal Irish Rifles joined the battalion.	

WAR DIARY
or
INTELLIGENCE SUMMARY.
(Erase heading not required.)

Army Form C. 2118.

Hour, Date, Place	Summary of Events and Information	Remarks and references to Appendices
1915	MAP REFERENCES – BELGIUM and FRANCE – SHEET – 36 – NO.000	
December 31st	In trenches at LE TOUQUET. About 9 am. enemy commenced shelling a dummy battery near LE TOUQUET Railway Station. About 30 (5.9) howitzer shells and 70 7.7mm shells fell in this locality. Strange to say a quiet day. Casualties One (1) Some heavy rifle fire was heard about 11 p.m. in front of 21st Div. on our right. See	[signature] Lt. Col. Comd. 2 R. Irish Rifles Comdg. 2 I.R. 1.1.16 2

74th Inf. Bde.

25th Division

2nd Battn.

ROYAL IRISH RIFLES

J A N U A R Y, 1 9 1 6.

J R Smith Rifles
Jan
Vol XIII

74 Bde 25th Div

Army Form C. 2118.

WAR DIARY
or
INTELLIGENCE SUMMARY.
(Erase heading not required.)

Instructions regarding War Diaries and Intelligence Summaries are contained in F.S. Regs., Part II. and the Staff Manual respectively. Title pages will be prepared in manuscript.

Hour, Date, Place	Summary of Events and Information	Remarks and references to Appendices
1916	MAP REFERENCES — BELGIUM & FRANCE — SHEET 36 — 1/40,000	
January 1ST	In trenches at LE TOUQUET – C10b. Quiet day. Casualties Nil	
2nd	In trenches as above. Very wet day, but quiet. Casualties Nil. 2ND LIEUT. John Stewart COCHRANE 18th (Service) Bn. Royal Irish Rifles joined the battalion.	
3rd	In trenches as above. About 11.30 am enemy shelled (about 30) Headquarter farm (SURREY FARM) C9.d.2.2. Not much damage done to the buildings, though the house was struck. Shelling continued in the afternoon chiefly in and around LE BIZET. Battalion was relieved by 15TH Cheshire Regiment. Relief complete 9.30 p.m. Casualties 1 KILLED. Battalion marched into billets at LE BIZET. Draft of 93 Other Ranks joined the battalion.	
4th	In billets at LE BIZET. Casualties Nil.	

JCJ

WAR DIARY
or
INTELLIGENCE SUMMARY.
(Erase heading not required.)

Army Form C. 2118.

Instructions regarding War Diaries and Intelligence Summaries are contained in F. S. Regs., Part II. and the Staff Manual respectively. Title pages will be prepared in manuscript.

Hour, Date, Place	Summary of Events and Information	Remarks and references to Appendices
	MAP REFERENCES — BELGIUM and FRANCE — SHEET 36 —	40,000
January 5th 1916	In billets at LE BIZET. Quiet day. Casualties Nil.	
" 6th	In billets as above. Casualties Nil. 2/Lt M. BENNETT Royal Irish Rifles joined	4
" 7th	In billets as above. Casualties 1 Wounded. Very slight.	7th Bde M. gun Coy
" 8th	Received during a firepose parade and the accidental	
	In billets as above. Relieved 13th Cheshire Regt-	
	In trenches at LE TOUQUET. Relief Complete 8 pm.	
	Casualties Nil.	
" 9th	In trenches as above. Quiet day. Casualties Nil	
" 10th	In trenches as above. Quiet day, except for	
	usual desultory shelling with 7.7 m.m rifle	
	Gun try bomb at no particular target. Casualties	
	2 other ranks wounded.	
" 11th	In trenches as above. Quiet day. Casualties 1 Other rank Wounded.	
" 12th	In trenches as above. Quiet day. Casualties 1 Other rank Wounded.	
" 13th	In trenches as above. Battalion relieved	
	by 13th Cho. Quiet day. Casualties Nil.	
	Y.S.N.	

Army Form C. 2118.

WAR DIARY
or
INTELLIGENCE SUMMARY.
(Erase heading not required.)

Instructions regarding War Diaries and Intelligence Summaries are contained in F.S. Regs., Part II. and the Staff Manual respectively. Title pages will be prepared in manuscript.

Hour, Date, Place	Summary of Events and Information	Remarks and references to Appendices
1916	MAP REFERENCES – BELGIUM and FRANCE – SHEET 36 – 1/40,000	
January 14th	In trenches at LE TOUQUET. Quiet day. Battalion was relieved by 13th Cheshire Regt. Relief complete at 7.30 p.m. Casualties 1 Wounded.	
15th	Br. Marched to billets at LE BIZET. In billets at LE BIZET. Quiet day. Casualties 1 Wounded (accidentally).	
16th	In billets at LE BIZET. Quiet day. Casualties 1 Wounded in action	
17th	In billets at LE BIZET. Quiet day. Casualties Nil.	
18th	In billets as above. Quiet day. Casualties Nil.	
19th	In billets as above. A minor Operation was carried out by a portion of the Battalion in front of the LE TOUQUET Salient. (C10 b) with the following objects:—	Ref. attached sketch tip
	I. To kill Germans.	
	II. To establish the identity of the enemy in the LE TOUQUET Salient.	
	III. To capture or destroy any enemy Machine guns in the LE TOUQUET Salient and MACHINE GUN HOUSE.	
	IV. To destroy any mine shaft found in the LE TOUQUET Salient.	

WAR DIARY
or
INTELLIGENCE SUMMARY.
(Erase heading not required.)

Army Form C. 2118.

MAP REFERENCES - BELGIUM and FRANCE - SHEET - 36 - 1/40,000.

Hour, Date, Place	Summary of Events and Information	Remarks and references to Appendices
January 19th 1916	(Cont.) In conjunction with the small assault - a gas attack under Divisional arrangements was launched against the enemy trenches about C.4.C. 9 in front of trenches 97 - 101 held by 9th Loyal North Lancashire Regt. but No actual assault was launched. This gas attack commenced at 4.30 pm and ceased about 5.15 pm and was most successfully carried out. At 4.35 pm a smoke attack commenced along the front of 91 Brigade (C.10 d 5.5) to C.4.c.9.6. and ceased finally at 5.5 pm. This attack shewed its advantage and disadvantage It produced an intense enemy bombardment and machine gun fire, but certainly helped at least one party to get arms to the German lines under Cover of the smoke. The artillery preparation commenced at 12.30 pm and ceased at 4.45 pm when the attack was launched.	(Trenches immediately N. of ours)

WAR DIARY
or
INTELLIGENCE SUMMARY.
(Erase heading not required.)

Army Form C. 2118.

Hour, Date, Place	Summary of Events and Information	Remarks and references to Appendices
1916	MAP REFERENCES - BELGIUM and FRANCE - SHEET 36 -	40,000
January 19th	(Cont) Its role was (a) to cut lanes through the German wire. (b) breach the enemy parapet at selected points of entry. (c) destroy CROWN PRINCE FARM (d) Counter battery fire. 18pr field guns - 9.2 and 6" Howitzers, 4.7 Howitzers and trench mortars (2" & 1½") were employed. The enemy retaliated almost immediately with artillery fire. Nine Officers and 220 men (inclusive of 2 Officers & other ranks R.E., who were to look for Mine Shafts - blow up Machine Gun Emplacements) and "Machine Gun parties") took part in the assault. The points of entry - marked A.B. and C. on attached sketch - were assaulted by two detachments. NORTHERN PARTY - (a) LEFT Party Point of Entry A. (b) RIGHT Party Point of Entry B. SOUTHERN PARTY - (a) 2 Officers, 90 Other ranks. Point of Entry C. The Northern and Southern party each had a	7 Officers 130 men

WAR DIARY or INTELLIGENCE SUMMARY.

Army Form C. 2118.

MAP REFERENCES – BELGIUM and FRANCE – SHEET 36 – 40,000

Hour, Date, Place	Summary of Events and Information	Remarks and references to Appendices
January 19th 1916	(Cont) "Headquarters and Liaison party" – included in above number) That the Northern Party in charge of LT. E. WORKMAN 5/R. Irish Rifles, and that of the Southern party under CAPTAIN H. IRELAND 3/Leinster Regt. Their role was to prepare the points of entry, pass them prisoners, And Not to return until all our attacking parties were back. The 13th Cheshire Regt. held the trenches during the attack. The attack commenced at 4.45 pm A few casualties occurred before the assault from enemy shell fire. The Northern and Southern parties attacked at the proper time and entered the enemy lines at the selected points of entry. The 13th Cheshire Regt. had on the Previous Night cut our wire. No obstacles were met either going to or coming back from the enemy lines. During the bombardment	

Army Form C. 2118.

WAR DIARY
or
INTELLIGENCE SUMMARY.
(Erase heading not required.)

Instructions regarding War Diaries and Intelligence Summaries are contained in F.S. Regs., Part II. and the Staff Manual respectively. Title pages will be prepared in manuscript.

Hour, Date, Place 1916	Summary of Events and Information	Remarks and references to Appendices
	MAP REFERENCES – BELGIUM and FRANCE – SHEET – 36 –	1/40,000
January 19th	(Cont) it was extremely difficult to trace the enemy trenches, which hith suffered considerably. The first German prisoner was there in our lines within five minutes of our assault commencing. The Northern party brought back 3 prisoners (including 1 Officer) and the Southern party brought lower 8 prisoners. The assault had divided into fresh dark hand-to-hand encounters accrued when the men mounted the parapet to assault. Many Germans were killed. The party detailed for CROWN PRINCE FARM were met by a strong party of Germans (about 50-70) at about 5.5 p.m. and our party did not reach its objective. This counter attack of the enemy appeared to lack determination. They only approached to within 50 x of our position.	

WAR DIARY
or
INTELLIGENCE SUMMARY.
(Erase heading not required.)

Army Form C. 2118.

Hour, Date, Place	Summary of Events and Information	Remarks and references to Appendices
	MAP REFERENCES – BELGIUM and FRANCE – SHEET-36 – 1/40,000	
19th January 1916	(Cont) and were fired at by a small party of our men (1 Officer and 4 men). Some were wounded. At 5.15 pm. Bugles were sounded as the signal to retire. No one appeared to hear the call, but as watches had been synchronised, and everyone was aware of the time of withdrawal, the parties fell back at this hour. The party whose objective was GERMAN MACHINE GUN House met with much opposition from grenades and rifle fire and did not reach its objective. No such shops were discovered in the enemy line. RED TILE House was reached, but some opposition was met from rifle fire and bombing from the ruins of this House. Enemy dugouts were bombed and many Germans killed. The prisoners	[C]

WAR DIARY
or
INTELLIGENCE SUMMARY.
(Erase heading not required.)

Army Form C. 2118.

Hour, Date, Place	Summary of Events and Information	Remarks and references to Appendices
1916	MAP REFERENCES - BELGIUM and FRANCE - SHEET - 36	
January 19th	(cont) belonged to 181ST Bavarian Rgt. The information gained - both from prisoners statements and captured documents was exceptionally valuable. The following Officers took part in the operation.	
	NORTHERN PARTY LT. E. Workman 5/R.I. Rifles. 2/LT. O'Rielly 4/R.I. Rifles. 2/LT. PHILLIPS 5/R.I. Rifles. 2/LT. Lennox 2/R.I. Rifles 2/LT. Brownfield 5/R.I. Rifles. and two R.E. Officers.	Southern party brought back 3 prisoners and Northern party 8 prisoners including 1 Unteroffizier. — 10,000
	SOUTHERN PARTY. Captain Ireland 3/Leinster Rgt. 2/LT. Cochrane 18th Royal Irish Rifles. LT. Cronine 3rd Royal Irish Rifles. The pluck, coolness and endurance of all ranks were magnificent. Casualties - Officers KILLED 2/LT. C.H. WALE 2/Royal Irish Rifles	

Army Form C. 2118.

WAR DIARY
or
INTELLIGENCE SUMMARY.
(Erase heading not required.)

Instructions regarding War Diaries and Intelligence Summaries are contained in F. S. Regs., Part II. and the Staff Manual respectively. Title pages will be prepared in manuscript.

Hour, Date, Place 1916	Summary of Events and Information	Remarks and references to Appendices
	MAP REFERENCES – BELGIUM and FRANCE – SHEET 36 – $\frac{1}{40,000}$	
19th January	(Capt) Cassidie MISSING, believed KILLED – 2/Lt. S. J. LENNOX 2/Royal Irish Rifles. WOUNDED 2/Lt. H PHILLIPS 5/R.I. Rifles. LT. E. WORKMAN 5/R.I. Rifles. 2/LT. W. H. O'REILLY 4/R.I. Rifles. 2/LT. A. A. BROOMFIELD 5/R.I. Rifles (slightly wounded; remained at duty) Other ranks Killed 9. Missing believed Killed 2 Wounded 57.	
20th January	In billets as above. Quiet day. 2/Lt. W.H. O'REILLY 4/R.I. Rifles died of wounds in the Field Ambulance. 2/Lt. A.A. Broomfield to hospital sick. Casualties Other ranks Nil.	
21st January	In billets as above. Battalion relieved 13th Cheshire Regt. in the trenches at LE TOUQUET. Casualties 1 Other rank wounded (accidentally) Draft 81 Other ranks joined the battalion.	
22nd January	In trenches as above. Quiet day. 1 Other rank Wounded.	
23rd January	In trenches as above. Quiet day. 2 Other ranks Wounded.	

WAR DIARY
or
INTELLIGENCE SUMMARY.
(Erase heading not required.)

Army Form C. 2118.

Hour, Date, Place	Summary of Events and Information	Remarks and references to Appendices
1916	MAP REFERENCES - BELGIUM and FRANCE - SHEET - 36 - 1/40,000	
January 24th	In trenches at LE TOUQUET. Quiet day. Casualties 2 Wounded	
25th	In trenches as above. Quiet day. Casualties Nil.	
26th	In trenches as above. Quiet day. Casualties Nil.	
27th	In trenches as above. Possibly owing to its being the Kaiser's birthday, the enemy shelled our front line and support trenches and their environs somewhat suddenly - Commencing about 4.30 am, increasing in violence about 10 am, and continuing in violence until 2 pm. LE TOUQUET Railway Station was shelled as well as Bn. H.Qrs. 77 mm and 10 cm. Shells were chiefly used. Few Casualties occurred. Bn. was relieved by 1/15th Cheshire Regt. Relief complete 9.15 pm. Battalion marched to billets in LE BIZET. Casualties Capt. D.B. de Alwnes BORCHERDS 4/Connaught Rangers Wounded. Other ranks 3 killed. 3 Wounded	3 killed 3 Wounded
28th	2 killed at LE BIZET. Quiet day. Casualties Nil.	

WAR DIARY
or
INTELLIGENCE SUMMARY.
(Erase heading not required.)

Army Form C. 2118.

MAP REFERENCES — BELGIUM and FRANCE — SHEET 36 — 1/40000

Hour, Date, Place 1916	Summary of Events and Information	Remarks and references to Appendices
January 29th	In billets at LE BIZET. Battalion was relieved by 11th H.L.I. The battalion marched off by companies during the morning and went into Divisional Rest at LA CRÈCHE	Military Cross awarded to Capt H R Ireland 3/Leinster Regt.
" 30th	A 5 d 7.8 2nd Lieut were billeted in farm houses etc. In billets as above. Lt T.S. Jenkinson 4/ Royal Irish Fusilier rejoined the battalion from hospital.	Lt E. Norman 5/R.I. Rifles. 2/Lt A.A. Broomfield 5/R.I. Rifles. D.C.M awarded to No 7752 Cpl H. Carthy 7174 Pte T. Trueman 10485 " R. Wilson all of to D.C.M 436 Pte W.J. Campbell
" 31st	In billets as above.	for gallantry on 19.1.16 (30.1.16)

J.C. Sprague Lt Col
(R. Irish Rifle
Comdg 2/R. Irish Rifles
31.1.16

74th Inf. Bde.

25th Division

2nd Battn.

ROYAL IRISH RIFLES,

FEBRUARY, 1916.

WAR DIARY
or
INTELLIGENCE SUMMARY.
(Erase heading not required.)

Army Form C. 2118.

S.D.O. 4/3 7/11/16

Hour, Date, Place	Summary of Events and Information	Remarks and references to Appendices
1916	MAP REFERENCES – BELGIUM and FRANCE – SHEET 36 – 40,000	
February 1st	Bn met billets at LA CRÊCHE A5d 7.8	Captain H L GIFFORD 2/R.I. Rifles struck off strength of Bn. (evac) wo letter of 31/1/16
2nd	Bn met billets as above	
3rd	Bn met billets as above	
4th	Bn met billets as above	
5th	Bn met billets as above	
6th	Bn met billets as above	
7th	Bn met billets as above	
8th	Bn met billets as above. 2/Lt T.H.W.DSTONE 4TH Bn. CONNAUGHT RANGERS joined the battalion	
9th	Bn billets as above. Bn paraded for route march and was inspected by G.O.C. 2ND ARMY.	
10th	Bn billets as above	
11th	Bn met billets as above	
12th	Bn met billets as above	
13th	Bn met billets as above	
14th	Bn met billets as above. Captain H. STANGER R.A.M.C. attached to battalion on relief of Captain W.E. BURROWS, R.A.M.C. hospital.	

L.S.

Army Form C. 2118.

WAR DIARY
or
INTELLIGENCE SUMMARY.
(Erase heading not required.)

Hour, Date, Place 1915	Summary of Events and Information	Remarks and references to Appendices
	MAP REFERENCES – BELGIUM and FRANCE – SHEET – 36 – 1/40,000.	
February 15th & 16th	In rest billets at LA CRÊCHE. A5 d 7.8.	
	In rest billets as above. Following Officers joined the battalion. 2LT J.A.GIBSON – 2LT J.CORDNER – 2LT J.L. MACLAUGHLIN – 2LT J.M.CLARKE – 2LT J.B.GETTY. All these Officers belong to 17th Bn. The ROYAL IRISH RIFLES (Service Bn.)	
17th	In rest billets as above. Draft of 53 Other ranks joined the battalion	18th R.I.Rifles
18th	In rest billets as above	
19th	In rest billets as above	
20th	In rest billets as above. 2LT J.S. COCHRANE to hospital sick.	
21st	In rest billets as above. LT F.J KING 3/Royal Irish Regiment to hospital sick	
22nd	In rest billets as above	
23rd	In rest billets as above	
24th	In rest billets as above. 2/LT F.J WHITE 2/8 R.I.Rifles "Permanent Base" and Others Officers rejoined Strength of Bn.	2/Lt Murrah F.S.

WAR DIARY
or
INTELLIGENCE SUMMARY.

(Erase heading not required.)

Army Form C. 2118.

Hour, Date, Place	Summary of Events and Information	Remarks and references to Appendices
1916	MAP REFERENCES – BELGIUM and FRANCE SHEET – 36 – 1/40,000	
February 25th	2. Divisional rest at LA CRÈCHE. A5 d 7.8	
26th	2. rest as above.	
27th	2. rest as above. 27 Other ranks joined the Battalion	
28th	2. rest billets as above.	
29th	2. rest billets as above. LT. C. T. PENTLAND R.A.M.C. attached to Bn in relief of Capt. H. STANGER R.A.M.C. who has definitely retired. LT W. E. BURROWS to hospital sick and evacuated).	

C Spopm Lt Col
Comdg 2/R Ind Rifles
2-3-16

74th Inf. Bde.

25th Division.

2nd. Battn.

ROYAL IRISH RIFLES,

MARCH, 1916.

Office of A.G.'s Office
Base   Secret

Herewith A.F.C 2118
(War Diary) for the month of
March 1916
            Please acknowledge
receipt

                    RECEIVED
                    for D.A.G., G.H.Q.,
                         3rd ECHELON.

                         Capt for
            G.S. Norman Lt-Col.
        Commdg 2/Bn The Royal Irish Rifles

[Stamp: 2nd BN. THE ROYAL IRISH RIFLES No. E4401]

WAR DIARY
or
INTELLIGENCE SUMMARY.

(Erase heading not required.)

Army Form C. 2118.

Hour, Date, Place	Summary of Events and Information	Remarks and references to Appendices
1916	MAP REFERENCES - BELGIUM and FRANCE - SHEET-36 - 1/40,000	
March 1st	In Divisional Rest at LA CRÈCHE - A.S.d. 7.8.	
2nd	In rest as above.	
3rd	In Rest billets as above	
4th	In rest billets as above	
5th	In rest billets as above	
6th	In rest billets as above. Battalion paraded 10 am and marched in brigade to VIEUX BERQUIN (By Map HAZEBROUCK 5A) in route south to join III Army - the XXV Division being transferred from II Corps to VIII Army - G.O.C. 2nd Corps inspected the battalion on (BAILLEUL - OUTTERSTEEN) road. 2/Lt. Captain de Courcy IRELAND 3/ Leinsters left to hospital sick	
7th	In billets at VIEUX BERQUIN.	
8th	In billets as above 2/Lt. G.W. PANTER - R.I. Rifles transferred as Observer (temporary) to R. Flying Corps.	

WAR DIARY
or
INTELLIGENCE SUMMARY.
(Erase heading not required.)

Army Form C. 2118.

Hour, Date, Place	Summary of Events and Information	Remarks and references to Appendices
1916	MAP REFERENCES – HAZEBROUCK 5A 1/100,000 and LENS 77 1/100,000	
March 9th	In rest billets at VIEUX BERQUIN	
10th	Battalion paraded 7.30 a.m. and marched to HAM EN ARTOIS and billeted there	
11th	In billets in HAM EN ARTOIS	
12th	Battalion paraded 9 a.m. and marched to BAILLEUL AUX CORNAILLES (Map ref. LENS II. 80000) and billeted there – two Companies billetted at MONCHY-BRETON.	
13th	In billets at BAILLEUL AUX CORNAILLES. Captain W.A. SMILES 17th Royal Irish Rifles joined the battalion	
14th	In billets as above. Battalion marched off at 9 a.m. to 17th Corps Area and billetted at ACQ. The battalion was attached to 139th Brigade for fatigue duties – chiefly carrying stores etc and work connected with munitions – in conjunction with the French, but in case of	

WAR DIARY
or
INTELLIGENCE SUMMARY.
(Erase heading not required.)

Army Form C. 2118.

Summary of Events and Information

MAP REFERENCES — LENS 11. — $\frac{1}{100,000}$

Hour, Date, Place 1916		Remarks and references to Appendices
March 14th	(Cont) Necessity the battalion turned he available for tactical purposes.	
March 15th	Battalion paraded at 9 am and moved to MONT ST. ELOY and billeted for the day in huts. The battalion details such as transport, Quartermasters etc remaining at A.C.Q. The battalion paraded at 6 pm. and marched by companies to support trenches about 900x NORTH of LA TARGETTE. And relieved 8th NOTTS and DERBY RGT.	
16th	In reserve trenches as above. The battalion found the necessary fatigue parties. Quiet day. A good deal of Hostile airplane activity noticeable during the day. LT. W.E. BURROWS R.A.M.C. returned to the battalion and relieved LT. C. PENTLAND R.A.M.C.	

JJ

WAR DIARY
or
INTELLIGENCE SUMMARY.

(Erase heading not required.)

Army Form C. 2118.

Hour, Date, Place	Summary of Events and Information	Remarks and references to Appendices
1916	MAP REFERENCES – LENS 11 – 100,000.	
March 17th	In Reserve trenches 900x N. of LA TARGETTE and E. of the BETHUNE Road. Quiet day.	
18th	In trenches as above. Quiet day except for a few shells falling near. 2ND LT. J.B. GETTY 17th Royal Irish Rifles was wounded. LT. MOSS 3/Royal Irish Rifles wounded slightly and remained at duty. Other ranks wounded 3. 2ND LT. W.WOODS joined the battalion having been given a Commission from 1st Class Mechanic in R. Flying Corps.	
19th	In trenches as above. Quiet day. Usual fatigues for mining Companies carried out. While reconnoitering the way from the Reserve trenches to reinforce the front line in case of attack by the enemy – LT. E.D. PRICE 41 R.I.Rgt. was wounded and died of wounds. Other ranks wounded one.	J.B. [signature] 19-3-16

WAR DIARY
or
INTELLIGENCE SUMMARY.
(Erase heading not required.)

Army Form C. 2118.

Hour, Date, Place 1916	Summary of Events and Information	Remarks and references to Appendices
	MAP REFERENCES – LENS –11– 100,000	
March 20th	In Reserve trenches 900x N. of LATARGETTE and E. of ROUTE DE BETHUNE. The usual mining. Fatigues were carried out. Casualties Other Ranks Nil	
21ST	In Reserve trenches as above. Quiet day except for about 20 6" H.E. shells falling near the Bethune Road. Casualties Nil	
22ND	In trenches as above. Quiet day. Captain H.R.H. IRELAND 3/Leinster Rgt. rejoined from hospital. Casualties Other Ranks KILLED - ONE.	
23rd	In trenches as above. Quiet day. Same heavy shells fell near BETHUNE ROAD. CAPTAIN H. D. McKAY 4/Connaught Rangers and 2/Lt. A.W. PAYNE 4/Connaught Rangers joined the Battalion.	
24th	In Trenches as above. Quiet day. Casualties Nil	
25th	In trenches as above. Quiet day. Casualties Nil	

WAR DIARY
or
INTELLIGENCE SUMMARY.
(Erase heading not required.)

Army Form C. 2118.

Hour, Date, Place	Summary of Events and Information	Remarks and references to Appendices
1916	MAP REFERENCES – LENS 11. 1/100,000	
March 25th (cont)	In reserve trenches about 900x N. of LATARGETTE and E. of BETHUNE ROAD. Quiet day. The battalion carried out the usual fatigues in conjunction with the 2nd Trench Running Companies. Casualties 1 Wounded	
26th	In trenches as above. Quiet day. Casualties	
27th	In trenches as above. Quiet day. The battalion was relieved by 11th Bn. The LANCASHIRE FUSILIERS. Relief complete about 11 pm. The battalion marched to billets at CHELERS. Casualties	
28th	In billets as above.	
29th	In billets as above.	
30th	In billets as above.	
31st	In billets as above.	

74th Inf. Bde.
25th Division.

2nd Battn.

ROYAL IRISH RIFLES,

A P R I L, 1 9 1 6.

WAR DIARY or INTELLIGENCE SUMMARY

Army Form C. 2118

APRIL 1916

Place	Date	Hour	Summary of Events and Information	Remarks and references to Appendices
CHELERS Sheet 36b 1/40,000 U.22.a	1.4.16	—	**MAP REFERENCES** FRANCE - SHEETS 36B + 51c 1/40,000 2ND BN. THE ROYAL IRISH RIFLES in billets at CHELERS. Sheet 36b. U.22.a. Usual field training was carried out. Casualties Nil	
	2.4.16	—	In billets as above. 2ND LT. E.N. WHITE 17th Bn. The Royal Irish Rifles and 2ND LT. D.O. TURPIN 17th Bn. The Royal Irish Rifles joined the battalion. Casualties Nil.	
	3.4.16	—	In billets as above. 2ND LT. T.H. GREY 5th Bn. The Royal Irish Rifles joined the battalion. Casualties Nil	
	4.4.16		In billets as above. Casualties Nil	
	5.4.16		In billets as above. Casualties Nil.	
	6.4.16		In billets as above. Casualties Nil.	
	7.4.16		In billets as above. Casualties Nil	

WAR DIARY
or
INTELLIGENCE SUMMARY

Army Form C. 2118

APRIL 1916

(Erase heading not required.)

Place	Date	Hour	Summary of Events and Information	Remarks and references to Appendices
			MAP REFERENCES — FRANCE - Sheets 36B & 51C	
CHELERS (36B) U22a	6.4.16		In billets at CHELERS. 2ND LT. W.W. VERNON 4/R.Ir.R. The Connaught Rangers and 2ND LT. P.E. MURRAY 4/R.Ir.R. The Connaught Rangers joined the battalion. Casualties Nil	
	9.4.16		In billets as above. Casualties Nil.	
	10.4.16		Battalion paraded about 9 am. and marched from CHELERS to new billets at TERNAS (sheet 51C) Bg d.	
TERNAS Bg d.	11.4.16		In billets as above	
	12.4.16		In billets as above. LT. W.E. BURROWS R.A.M.C. proceeded to England, having finished two years service. Captain R.N. VAISEY R.A.M.C. joined the battalion for duty.	
	13.4.16		In billets as above	
	14.4.16		In billets as above. 2LT. A.G. MITCHELL 5/Royal Irish Rifles joined the battalion	

Army Form C. 2118

WAR DIARY or INTELLIGENCE SUMMARY

(Erase heading not required.)

APRIL 1916

Instructions regarding War Diaries and Intelligence Summaries are contained in F.S. Regs., Part II. and the Staff Manual respectively. Title Pages will be prepared in manuscript.

Place	Date	Hour	Summary of Events and Information	Remarks and references to Appendices
TERNAS (51st) Bga.			MAP REFERENCES FRANCE- SHEETS 36B and 51C / 40,000	
	15.4.16		In billets at TERNAS.	
	16.4.16		In billets as above.	
	17.4.16		In billets as above. LT GRANT-MORRIN R.A.M.C. joined the battalion, relieving LT MASSEY R.A.M.C.	
	18.4.16		In billets as above.	
	19.4.16		In billets as above. 2/LT. C. BRADDEL 5/Royal Irish Rifles joined the battalion	
	20.4.16		In billets as above. LT. GRANT-MORRIN R.A.M.C. to hospital sick. 2LT. C.V. SMILEY 4/Royal Irish Rifles joined the battalion.	
	21.4.16		In billets as above. LT. MASSEY R.A.M.C. joined the battalion for duty. 2LT. T.H.F. SHARKEY 4/Royal Irish Rifles joined the battalion.	
	22.4.16		In billets as above. The battalion paraded at 1pm. and at 2 pm. proceeded by motor 'bus to – Sheet 51C – E.6.5.7.7 and marched to trenches at and relieved 4th Leicestershire Rgt. in trenches 86,87,88, and 89. Relief complete 5.40 am. 23.4.16 above map reference 36C / 40,000 S 22	

Army Form C. 2118

WAR DIARY
or
INTELLIGENCE SUMMARY

(Erase heading not required.)

APRIL 1916.

Place	Date	Hour	Summary of Events and Information	Remarks and references to Appendices
			MAP REFERENCES FRANCE - SHEET - 36C	
S.22	23.4.16		In trenches at S.22. Trenches here very wet. A certain amount of shelling took place, principally on the front line. The enemy were very active with Trench Mortars and caused some casualties with their Mortars and Rifle Grenades. WOUNDED Slightly and remained at duty. 2/LT. P.E. MURRAY 4/Connaught Rangers. Other ranks KILLED 4, WOUNDED 23	
Trenches Plugs-	24.4.16		In trenches as above. The situation was normal during the day, but heavy shelling, Minenwerfer and bombs were directed on to our trenches unceasingly. Casualties 1 Other rank Wounded.	
Street	25.4.16		In trenches as above. The enemy exploded a mine at about 1.30 p.m. on the immediate right of the sector held by the Battalion, but first of this we had. The enemy occupied it at once, but up Lewis guns etc. and finally consolidated it. The usual shell fire and minenwerfer fire continued throughout the day. The trenches	

WAR DIARY / INTELLIGENCE SUMMARY

Army Form C. 2118

APRIL 1916   FRANCE - SHEET 36C

Place	Date	Hour	Summary of Events and Information	Remarks and references to Appendices
Trenches S.22	25.4.16		(Continued) were very heavy but our casualties somewhat damaged. Casualties 2/Lt. H.E. WHITE 17/Royal Irish Rifles wounded. Lt. A. MASSEY R.A.M.C. wounded, remained on duty. Other ranks 4 wounded. 2/Lt. E.B.K. LOYD R.I. Rifles joins the battalion.	
	26.4.16		2 Trenches as above. About 3.40 a.m. a mine was exploded by the enemy on our left, & he occupied it and consolidated his position during the day. When the mine was exploded he lifted his trench and temporarily occupied about 100 four trenches but greater than almost immediately re-occupied our trench a few moments later, but was bombed out, and our line was re-occupied by us. The New Mine was consolidated during the day by the enemy. The usual minenwerfer and shell fire was directed onto our trenches by the enemy. Casualties - KILLED 2/Lt. H.W.D. STONE 4/Connaught Rifles - Other ranks 3 2 W. WOUNDED 2/Lt. T.H. GREY 5/Royal Irish 7K Other ranks also Lt. J.S. JENKINSON 4/R. Irish Fusilier Lt. T.J.C. THOMPSON 4/Royal Irish Fusilier (the latter remained)	

WAR DIARY

INTELLIGENCE SUMMARY

Army Form C. 2118

April 1916

Map References: FRANCE - SHEET 36C

Place	Date	Hour	Summary of Events and Information	Remarks and references to Appendices
Trenches about S22	27.4.16		In trenches as above. Usual trench mortar and artillery activity on the part of the enemy. Casualties - Captain G.S. NORMAN 2/R.I. Rifles and LT. P. MOSS 3/Royal Irish Rifles, both slightly, and remain at duty. The battalion was relieved by 15th Cheshire Regt, but left two Lewis Guns and teams to remain in the line. Relief complete about 3.40 a.m. 28.4.16. On relief Companies marched back to meet at CAMBLAIN L'ABBE' (Sheet 36B - W22) arriving there about 9 am 28.4.16	
Camblain l'abbé	28.4.16		On meeting at CAMBLAIN L'ABBE - about 8.15 p.m. orders came for the battalion to "Stand to" and proceed to CABARET ROUGE (36C - S13d 6.8). The battalion moved off within 10 minutes and arrived there at CABARET ROUGE 12.15 am on 29.4.16. The situation was then normal again, but previously during the night the enemy had opened a rifle	
CABARET ROUGE S13d 78 Sheet 36C				

WAR DIARY
or
INTELLIGENCE SUMMARY

(Erase heading not required.)

Army Form C. 2118

APRIL 1916

Place	Date	Hour	Summary of Events and Information	Remarks and references to Appendices
			MAP REFERENCES FRANCE - Sheet 36c 1/40,000	
Cabaret Rouge S.13.d.7.8. Sheet 36c.	28.4.16		(Cont) Mine on the front of 7th Bde exter and the situation had not been abnormal. The Battalion remained at CABARET ROUGE until 3 a.m. when three Companies returned to CAMBLAIN L'ABBÉ.	
Camblain l'Abbé W.22 Sheet 36A	29.4.16		Bn now at CAMBLAIN L'ABBÉ (Sheet 36B - W 2 2)	
	30.4.16		Bn now at CAMBLAIN L'ABBÉ. Fourth Company rejoined Battalion.	

[signature] Lt Col
1/10th R.Lpl R/b
Comdg 1/10th R.Lpl R/b
1.5.16.

74th Inf. Bde.

25th Division.

2nd Battn.

ROYAL IRISH RIFLES,

MAY, 1916.

> A.G.'s OFFICE AT THE BASE.
> War Diaries & Records.
> DATE 3/5/16
> C. R. No. 8700/352

Subject:- Duplicate War Diaries.

To:- OC
2 R Irish Rifles

The enclosed Duplicate War Diary is returned to you please, as "Duplicates" are not required in this Office, vide:- General Routine Order, No. 1125.

G.H.Q.,
3rd Echelon,
3/5/1916.

Major,
for D. A. G.

2/1/1154 R1-4

Army Form C. 2118

WAR DIARY
or
Intelligence Summary

Place $\frac{1}{2}$ X 36b40,000

Summary of events and information France-Sheet 36c.& 36b40,000

Place	Date	Map References	Summary of events and information
CABIN LABBE W22(36b)	1/5/16		Resting in billets, Casualties NIL, Strength 31 Officers 930 Other Ranks
"	2/5/16		Resting in billets as above
"	3/5/16		Resting in billets as above. The Battalion paradedd at 7.15 p.m. and relieved 13th Cheshire Regt.
Trenches S.22 (36c)			In trenches -Q.Sector,trenches 86-89 inclusive,about S22(36c. 2/Lieut.W.Wood 2/Royal Irish Rifles to hospital sick (4-5-16)
"	4/5/16		In trenches as above.Quiet day .Casualties 1 Other Rank wounded
"	5/5/16		In trenches as above Quiet day till 7.45 p.m. The Germans commenced a bomb attack on Q.89 and Q.90.A red light was sent up and the enemy shelled very heavily.They were vigorously shelled and bombed in reply. Casualties 5K. 12.W. Lieut.P.Erskine 3/R.I.Rifles to C.C.S. from 74/1 T. Mortar Battery. Strength 30 Officers 912 Otherv Ranks
"	6/5/16		Quiet Day
"	7/5/16		Quiet day The Battalion worked continously at trenches which were very bad.Lieut.Massey R.A.M.C., relieved by Lieut. Hesterton R.A.M.C..
"	8/5/16		Quiet Day.
"	9/5/16		Quiet day. At 7.45 p.m.two large mines were sprung on our left in the Lines of 9th L.N.Lancs. A struggle ensued for craters in which 9th L.N.L. were generally sucessful.Our left company was able to lend much assistance by supplying bombs etc.About 2.30 a.m.the 13th Cheshire Regt. relieved the Battalion and the latter went into Brigade Reserve.2½ Coys in ZOUAVE VALLEY and 1½ Companies at CABARET ROUGE,Casualties 2 wounded.
Zouave Valley and CABARET ROUGE	10/5/16		In Brigade Reserves as above.Much shelling on the Sector on our left about 7.30 p.m. Strength Officers 31.Other Ranks 895.
"	11/5/16		In Bde Reserve.Lieut. Hesterton R.A.M.C..relieved by Lieut A.J.E.LINGEY R.A.M.C. Quiet day Casualties Nil.
"	12/5/26		In Brigade Reserve as above Quiet day Casualties Nil
"	13/5/16		In Brigade Reserve as above .The enemy shelled the valley continously during the day.At 7.14 p.m. the Germans sprang a mine about 70x.in front of the near lip of the crater.at the request of the O.C. 13th Q.88,the 13th Cheshire Regt. occupied the near lip of the crater.at the request of the O.C. 13th Cheshires Regt. two platoons were sent up to reinforce the garrison of Q.88 On he return they

WAR DIARY

Intelligence Summary

Summary of events and information France-Sheet 36c and 36b $\frac{1}{40,000}$

Army Form C.2118

Place	Date	Map Reference	
Zouave Valley & Cabaret Rouge	13/5/16.	B.22 (36c)	they came under a intensely heavy fire and with difficulty a portion of reached Q.88 By 3.40 a.m. 14-5-16 Q.88 was taken over from the 13th Cheshire Regiment. Casualties "2/Lieut.A.G.Mitchell 17/R.I.Rifles KILLED,2/Lieut H.E.White 5/R.I.Rifles wounded 2/Lieut J.H.F. Sharkey wounded remained at duty.Other ranks K.3. W. 14
	14/5/16		In Brigade reserve, Quiet day Casualties.
	15/5/16		In Brigade reserve. Q.87 and Q.88 were taken over from the 13th Cheshire Regt.During the day the enemy shelled the ZOUAVE VALLEY at intervals with shells of varying calibres About 8.3 0.pm. 2 mines were sprung in front of the Battalion and our left (i.e.9th.L.N.L. and detachments of the 11th Lancashire Fusiliers occupied the crater.The enemy put up the usual barrage fire which was chiefly heaviest in the Battalion sector on our left Casualties K.3. Wounded 12.
	16/5/16		About 1.30 a.m. the crater in front of Q.88 was taken over from the 13th Cheshire Regt. During the day the enemy shelled the front and support lines with Minne werfers and shells of 7.7 up to 8"". The trenches and communication trenches were somewhat damaged a great deal of work was done by us including the communication trenches leading up to the new crater in front of Q.88 the crater being already full consolidated. Quiet night Strength Total 2 8 Officers 958 Other Ranks Fighting 24 " 580 "
	17/5/16		In trenches Q.86-Q.89 The enemy knocked in the Majority of trenches and communication trenches with shells and trench mortars.About ll.am. the enemy commenced a bombing attack on M the crater.88 This was repulsed until 1.25 p.m. when owing to casualties, the supply of bombs giving out and reinforcements not arriving in time the surviving officer and two men out of a garrison of 24 retired and established themselves in a sap head leading from the main fire trench A lewis gun and one man had previously been sent away from crater a Counter attack was ordered to take place at 9.pm.Owing to the necessarily hurried arrangementsAlenAndual condition of the trenches the lack of "pumping Off" accomodation the attack became disorganised and failed The Artillery preparation had lasted at intervals from 6.pm. til 1 9.p.m.

W A R D I A R Y
or
Intelligence Summary

Army Form C.2118

Place	Date	Map References	Summary of events and Information France-Sheet -36c
Trenches S.22 (36 c)	17-5-16		The crater was very strongly held by the enemy with bombs and Machine Gun A second attack was organised. XXXXXXXXXXXXXXXXXXXXXXXX but owing to instructions received from Higher authority that, should the objective be too difficult and the chances of success slight, it was not to take place. This being the case the second assault was cancelled. Total casualties Killed 16 wounded 73 Missing 5.
	18-5-16		In trenches as above. Throughout the day the enemy bombarded with shells and trench mortars the trenches occupied by the battalion. Many places were badly damaged and casualties inflicted. Instr Battalion reliefs were effected Casualties NIL.
	19-5-16.		In trenches the enemy continued his bombardment of the trenches with trench mortars and shells The Battalion was relieved by the 1/7 London Regiment (Territorials). Relief complete about 12.30 a.m. 20-5-16. The relief was delayed owing to the 10th Cheshire Regt. on the right (7th Bde) attacking and capturing a crater and the incidental enemy bombardment was allowed to subside first. The Battalion proceeded to billets at ACQ It appeared that the enemy activity during the last three days possibly might have been do ne to a purpose i.e. testing our strength. Casualties K.7. W. 14.
	20-5-16		In billets at ACQ. The Battalion paraded at 8.45 p.m. and proceeded via AUBIGNY and FENIN to AVERDOINGT and arrived at that place at about 3-10 a.m. 21-5-16 where the Battalion billeted.
AVERDOINGT	21-5-16		In billets at AVERDOINGT 2/Lieut.J.Watson 3/R.I.Rifles and 2/Lieut T.Barton 4/R.I.Rifles joined the Battalion.
	22-5-16		In billets as above. About 7 a.m. an urgent message arrived ordering the Battalion to BAILLEUL AUX CORNAILLERS where the Brigde . was concentrating. The Battalion arrived there about 8. a.m. It was understood that the enemy had made an attack on the sector which the Battalion had vacated on 19-5-16 After remaining at BAILLEUL AUX CORNAILLES until 12 noon the Battalion was sent back to AVERDOINGT having previously despatched three Officers and eight N.C.Os to act as guides to the 99th Brigade who were to effect a relief to-night
	23-5-16		In billets as above 2/Lieut P Windle 4/R.I.Rifles and 2/Lieut S.A.Bell 2/R.I.Rifles joined the Battalion. 2/Lieut J.CORDNER is 17th R.I.Rifles to Field Ambulance (Shell Shock) 7 other ranks joined the Battalion.

WAR DIARY
or Intelligence Summary

Army Form C.2118

France Sheet 51 c 1/40,000

Place	Date	Map References	Summary of events and information
Averdoingt	24/5/16		In billets at AVERDOINGT
"	25/5/16		In billets as above Captain Massey R.A.M.C. rejoined the Battalion, relieving Lt Tingey R.A.M.C. 2/Lieut H.E.White 17/R.I.Rifles evacuated to England
"	26/5/16		In billets as above
"	27/5/16		In billets as above 2/Lieut Grey to F.A. from U.K.
"	28/5/16		In billets as above 2/Lieut. Gordner to U.K.
"	29/5/16		In billets as above Capt. W.Smiles 17/R.I.Rifles to Field Ambulance /Lieut.Braddel
"	30/5/16		In billets as above ,12 other ranks joined the Battalion. to Field Ambulance.sick
"	31/5/16		In billets as above .Battalion paraded about Noon and proceeded tto billets at BAILLEUL AUX CORNAILLES. Lieut.G.F.L.Murphy R.A.M.C. joined the Battalion relieving Captain Massey, 2/Lieut C. Edwards 4/R.I.Rifles to Field Ambulance ,sick.

D.A.G.
3rd Echelon
Base.

With reference to the attached
War Diary of 2nd Bn. The Royal
Irish Rifles for the months of
February and March 1916
I beg to report that the duplicate
War diary for these months
was not sent to you, but
was forwarded to the Officer
i/c Records No 11 District Dublin.
who acknowledged the receipt
of them.
In view of this I am returning
the Original War Diary for
February and March 1916 to you.

15.5.16

L C Sprague
Lt. Col.
Cmdg. 2/R.I. Rifles.

74th Inf. Bde.

25th Division.

2nd Battn.

ROYAL IRISH RIFLES,

J U N E, 1 9 1 6.

2 R Irish Rifles
2 R Irish Rifles 1916 1 of 18

WAR DIARY
or
INTELLIGENCE SUMMARY

Army Form C. 2118

JUNE ~~MAY~~ 1916

19.

Place	Date	Hour	Summary of Events and Information	Remarks and references to Appendices
			MAP REFERENCES FRANCE Sheet 51C & 36 40,000	
	1.6.16		In Billets at BAILLEUL AUX CORNAILLES P.O. Opaque Sheet 51C/11/5 to 9 9/10	
	2.6.16		In billets as above. Coy & C. known to B. H.Q. 2 5/16	
	3.6.16		In billets — as above. C/R O'Meara left, proceed to Base.	
	4.6.16		In billets — as above.	
	5.6.16		In billets — as above.	
	6.6.16		In billets — as above. The Strength of Officers (C/Dy a.o. & killing) Lt Colonel G.B.F. Smith from Base rejoined Lt Coster 360 men for RCJ joined from F.A.	

WAR DIARY
or
INTELLIGENCE SUMMARY

(Erase heading not required.)

Army Form C. 2118

FRANCE / LENS

Place	Date	Hour	Summary of Events and Information	Remarks and references to Appendices
			(illegible handwritten entries)	

WAR DIARY
or
INTELLIGENCE SUMMARY
(Erase heading not required.)

Army Form C. 2118

Place	Date	Hour	Summary of Events and Information Army of FRANCE 1/100,000 LENS 11	Remarks and references to Appendices
BRUAY	June 1	—	Billet — Lt Col U Smyth to 25th Division. D. Left Col shot to Major a Smart	Lt Col ...
	3	—	Billet. Strength 37 Officers ... and total O.R. 916 O.R.ank	Major
	4	—	Dett. Run marched to ÉCOURES. Lt Smyth rejoined Bttln	otherwise
ÉCOURES	5	—	Marched to MAIZICOURT (near AUXI-LE-CHATEAU)	
	6	—	In Billets ~ above	
MAIZICOURT	7	—	Marched to FRANSU. Various orders from ... O.R.s ... fell out. Lt Williams from front SOS	

WAR DIARY
or
INTELLIGENCE SUMMARY
(Erase heading not required.)

Army Form C. 2118

FRANCE July 1917 LENS II Corps

Place	Date	Hour	Summary of Events and Information	Remarks and references to Appendices
FRANCE				
ST LEGER near PROUART	19		Handed to ST LEGER (nr DOMART) Night Reveille	
ST LEGER	20		In billets ST LEGER. L.P. Erskine struck off strength T.M. 25 O.R. joined	
	21		In billets	
	21		In billets. Strength 38 Officers (incl M.O. & Chaplain) 930 O.R. L.t Pagae appointed from leave 825 O.R. 750 O.R. Feeding Trench 29"	
	22		In billets	
	23		Billets and other Battalions nr Brigade were counting race	
			Moved to CANAPLES (10 P.m.)	

Army Form C. 2118

WAR DIARY
or
INTELLIGENCE SUMMARY
(Erase heading not required.)

Instructions regarding War Diaries and Intelligence Summaries are contained in F. S. Regs., Part II. and the Staff Manual respectively. Title Pages will be prepared in manuscript.

Army of FRANCE / LENS 11

Place	Date	Hour	Summary of Events and Information	Remarks and references to Appendices
CANAPLES	June 25th		Marched to BONNEVILLE arrived 6 p.m.	G.M.Y.Cie. [illegible]
BONNEVILLE	26"		Batt'n. Major E. T. Burke O.C. 1 40 O.R's arrived	Each when Others were sick
"	27"		Batt'n. Strength 37 Officers 1 M.O. 1 Chaplain 971 O.R's	
"	28"		Batt'n. marched to MIRVAUX arrived 2 a.m. 29"	
MIRVAUX	29"		Bath. The Bn. now billeted in 15 minutes and can move off easily in 30 minutes.	
"	30"		Batt'n. marched to HARPONVILLE 6.30 p.m. Batt'n. arrived 7h30. Fighting Strength 36 Officers, 1 Chaplain 1028 O.R's	

J. Thompson Lt. Colonel
O/C 7/R. I. Rif.

1/July/1916

74th Bde.
25th Div.

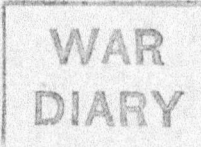

2nd BATTALION

The ROYAL IRISH RIFLES.

JULY 1916

VOLUME XXIII
WAR DIARY or INTELLIGENCE SUMMARY 1916

12th R. Rifles 25 July
Army Form C. 2118
Rough Reference. FRANCE — LENS
Vol 19

July

Place	Date	Hour	Summary of Events and Information	Remarks and references to Appendices
HARPONVILLE	July 1st		In Billets. Strength 36 Officers + 2 attached, 1028 O.R's (M.O. Chaplain)	Casualties as under, unless specially specified 14/25
SENLIS	2nd		In Billets.	
SENLIS	3rd		Marched to BOUZINCOURT at 9.30 pm, where Bn. bivouacked.	
BOUZINCOURT	4th		From bivouac to billets 6pm. 2 Lt T.H. Galwey (3rd R.IR.) & 2 Lt W.L.P. Dobbin (3rd R.IR.) joined the Bn.	
BOUZINCOURT	5th		In billets.	
BOUZINCOURT	6th	2.30 pm	Marched through ALBERT and bivouacked about half a mile E. of it, until 11 pm, when the Bn (Strength 20 Officers + 603 other ranks) proceeded to assembly trenches at LA BOISSELLE preparatory to an attack near tournans.	
LA BOISSELLE	7th		Active operations. At 8 am the Bn. occupied trenches on the line X.14.a.2.8. to X.14.d.4.7. vacated by the 9th L.N. LANCS. (Right) and 13th CHESHIRES (Left) which had gone	

WAR DIARY
or
INTELLIGENCE SUMMARY

(Erase heading not required.)

Army Form C. 2118

Place	Date	Hour	Summary of Events and Information	Remarks and references to Appendices
	7th on 8th		Forward in the attack. A & B Coys: behind 13th CHESHIRES and C & D Coy behind 9th L.N.LANCS. At 9.50am K.O.R.L. (Kings Own Royal?) and occupied the line X14 a 66. to X14 d 82. Casualties on this day were: Shed 7148 X14692 P C Pulls	
			Officers killed: 2Lt W.W. VERNON. CONN: RANGERS.	
			2Lt J. WATSON. R.I. RIFLES.	
			Wounded: CAPT. H.R.H. IRELAND 3rd LEINSTER REGT.	
			Lieut. W.R. MOSS 3rd R. I RIFLES	
			2nd Lt J.L. MacLAUGHLIN R.I. RIFLES	
			2nd Lt C. WEIR R.I. RIFLES.	
			2nd Lt C.E. WILSON R.I. RIFLES.	
			Other ranks: Killed 28	
			Wounded 116	
			Missing 17	
			This line was held throughout the day.	

WAR DIARY or INTELLIGENCE SUMMARY

Army Form C. 2118

2nd R. Rifles

Date	Hour	Summary of Events and Information	Remarks and references to Appendices
8th		Until 6pm remained in position captured on 7th. A Coy brought from left flank to right flank & took remainder of 9 R.I. Rif Bn + 2 Coys of 11 Lanc. Fus. were ordered to advance in touch from X.14.b. 2.85. to X.14.b. 7.0.; but through difficulty in identifying points the face nearly reached the X.9.d.2 to X.9.c.4.4. which had been given as the objective to be gained by a night attack. At 8.40 p.m. the attack was launched, 11 Coys + 9 Lanc. Fus. followed by 2 R.I. Rifles. and position was taken up in trench X.9.d. 5.2.87 to X.9.d. 5.2.11. The LSR all night to Consolidate. As the Bn. had too far forward, (no enemy) there was no counter-attack on troops on the right and left. During the night and during the day of the 9th our troops in this position were subject to a continuous barrage from our own artillery, owing to difficulty of communication were unaware of our presence in that position. 2Lt J.F. Shein (3 R.I.R.) joined Bn.	
9th		About 4 p.m. the enemy, massing in the factory from Continuation Wood attacked, & outflanking us, which forces to retire to original	

R.I. Rifles

WAR DIARY
or
INTELLIGENCE SUMMARY
(Erase heading not required.)

Army Form C. 2118

Place	Date	Hour	Summary of Events and Information	Remarks and references to Appendices
Cults	9/15		Objective at X9c82. X9a44. Rels by a company of Lanc Fus. with the 8th N. Staffords on the right, about X.15.6.1.0. The enemy trenches "Vigorous" & the retirement was carried out in good order. The casualties on this day were. Officers. Killed. Capt W.A. Smiles. R.I.Rif. Wounded. 2Lt P.E. Murray. 4. Conn. Rang. 2Lt P. Windle. R.I.Rif. 2Lt J.M. Clarke. R.I.Rif. O. Ranks— Killed. 12 Wounded. 62 Missing. 45. Casualties of previous day. Officers. Killed. Lt W.C. McConnell. 3 R.I.Rif. Wounded 2Lt P. McMahon. R.I.Rif. 2Lt D.O. Turpin. R.I.Rif. Other Ranks. K. 7 W. 22 M. 11	

WAR DIARY
or
INTELLIGENCE SUMMARY
(Erase heading not required.)

Army Form C. 2118

2nd R. Rifles

Place	Date	Hour	Summary of Events and Information	Remarks and references to Appendices
	10th		The Bn. was relieved by the 8th L.N. Lancs in the early hours of the morning & marched to SENLIS via ALBERT & BOUZINCOURT, arriving at SENLIS at 9 a.m. where we bivouacked until 8.30 p.m. We then went into billets.	
SENLIS	11th		In billets. Maj. J. Evans. R. Innis. Fus: joined B.n. & Capt. Liv. 22nd in Command.	
SENLIS	12th		In billets.	
SENLIS	13th		In billets.	
	14th		Marched from SENLIS through BOUZINCOURT to USNA HILL trenches. Arrived at 8 p.m. relieved the 11th Cheshires at 2 p.m. and took over trenches from X.8.c.6.2 to X.8.c.3.4. with B.C. from A. C & D Coys in front line from X.14 & 9.b.	
	15th		Left USNA HILL at 2 p.m. and took over fire trenches from 11th Cheshires about X.14 & 9.b. until opposed other coys at 11 p.m. Casualties other ranks Killed 2. Wounded 3. P.T.W. 22d	

Instructions regarding War Diaries and Intelligence Summaries are contained in F.S. Regs., Part II. and the Staff Manual respectively. Title Pages will be prepared in manuscript.

Army Form C. 2118

WAR DIARY
or
INTELLIGENCE SUMMARY
(Erase heading not required.)

Place	Date	Hour	Summary of Events and Information	Remarks and references to Appendices
TRENCHES (OVILLERS)	JULY 16th		At 12.20 A.M. the Battalion in conjunction with 2 Coys of the 13th CHESHIRE REGT. took part in a night attack. At 1 a.m. the attack was launched. Its objective allotted to the Bn. being X 8 c 5.6. (incl.) to X 8 c 2.4. (excl.) The Bn. formed up in 6 lines in a half company front, in the following order. D-A-C-B Coy. remaining as trench garrison. The foremost line reached the enemy's wire, but owing to very heavy machine gun fire (from front and from the right of our own trench, which was held by the enemy) were forced to return. From 9 A.M. to 4 P.M. an enemy bombing post about X 6 8.4.) but only progress 10 yds. in half time a new hurricane being contemplated. In preparing, weakened by considerable casualties were reinforced by 2 squads of the Lancs. Fus. Grenadiers. A further bombing attack was again considered and they must j with Grenadiers, which succeeded in dislodging at about 7 pm. Hut we captured (Captain, 1 Lieut & 126 other ranks of the 15th Regt	Map Ref. Sheet 57d SE 1/20,000

H. I. Ruffin

WAR DIARY
or
INTELLIGENCE SUMMARY

(Erase heading not required.)

Army Form C. 2118

Place	Date	Hour	Summary of Events and Information	Remarks and references to Appendices
OVILLERS (TRENCHES)	16/15		During the bombing operations No. 9641 Cpl. READING 2. R. Ir. RIFLES specially distinguished himself. This successful operation enabled the Bn. to secure the South-Eastern perimeter of OVILLERS. The right flank of the Bn. linking up with the 5/15 ROYAL WARWICKSHIRE REGT. The Bn. was relieved by 6/15 R. WAR. WICKSHIRE REGT. at about 12 m.n. CASUALTIES. OFFICER KILLED. 2LT J. LECKY. OFFICERS WOUNDED SGT. F.M. GREENLEY. CAPT. D.H. KELLY. 2LT T.N. GALLWEY. 2LT R.A. BENNETT. (13TH CLASH; ATT. 2.R.IR.) OFFICER MISSING. 2LT T.E. BARTON. OTHER RANKS. KILLED. 2 WOUNDED. 42 MISSING. 6	

WAR DIARY
or
INTELLIGENCE SUMMARY

Army Form C. 2118

2 R.A. Rifles

Place	Date	Hour	Summary of Events and Information	Remarks and references to Appendices
Bouzincourt	17th		Battalion arrived a Bouzincourt at about 6.30 a.m. and went into huts. At 5.30 p.m. the Bn. marched to Forceville where at bivouacked.	
	18th		Marched from Forceville to Beauval at 8 a.m. where Bn. billetted.	
Beauval	19th		Inspection of Bde. by G.O.C. Division, who congratulated Bde. on its good work around La Boisselle and at Ovillers.	
" "	20th		In billets.	
Beauval	21st		Marched to Brigade at 9.10 a.m. to Bus les Artois where Bn. went into huts. 2 Lt. J.R. Tuckett (2 R.I.R.) joined Bn. 2 Lt. Gt. Pry. (3 R.I.R.) " " 2 Lt. F.C. Knox (4 R.I.R.) " " 158 other ranks joined Bn.	
Bus les Artois	22nd		In huts.	
"	23rd		In huts. 43 " " " "	
"	24th		Marched to Mailly-Maillet Wood at 10 a.m. Bn. took over trenches (Right subsector held by 74th Bde. Q.17.a.6.4. Serre Redan3 to Q.16.b.37.) from the 1st Bn. R. Innis. Fus. at 4 p.m. Q.17.a. R. Crowley. 3 Leins: R. Q.16. G.D. Jones. R. Fowler. 429 O.R. joined Bn.	

WAR DIARY or INTELLIGENCE SUMMARY

Army Form C. 2118

2/0 R.S. Ryfs

Place	Date	Hour	Summary of Events and Information	Remarks and references to Appendices
TRENCHES	25 26 27 28 29		25th 2/Lt C.R. COONEY (R.D.F.) } 29 Other ranks joined Bn. 2/Lt. J.J. DALY (2 Leins: R.) } Casualties during tour:- OFFICERS NIL O.R. 19 wounded	Reference Map Sheet 57DSE 1/ 20000
MAILLY MAILLET WOOD	30th		Relieved 6 a.m. by the 13th Cheshire Regt. the Bn. marching into camp not in MAILLY-MAILLET WOOD (P.18 central). 37 Other ranks joined Bn. In Camp.	
MAILLY MAILLET WOOD	31st		In Camp.	

P. 18. central

31. 7. 16.

L. Sharpe Lieut Colonel
Comdg 2/Royal Irish Rifles

74th Brigade.

25th Division.

2nd B BATTALION

ROYAL IRISH RIFLES

AUGUST 1916

Volume 1. 9th Royal Irish Rifles Vol 20

WAR DIARY
or
INTELLIGENCE SUMMARY 1916
AUGUST

Place	Date	Hour	Summary of Events and Information	Remarks and references to Appendices
MAILLY MAILLET WOOD	1st		Battalion in huts at MAILLY MAILLET WOOD Strength 28 Officers 791 O.R.	Map Reference Sheet 57D SE 1/20,000
	2nd		" " "	
	3rd		" " "	
	4th		" " "	Draft of 9 O.R. joined the Bn.
	5th		Battalion relieved about mid-day by 9th Norfolk Regt. and marched to Camp at BERTRANCOURT. Draft of 29 O.R. joined the Battalion.	57 D 1/40,000
	6th		Camp at BERTRANCOURT. Lt.G. Calwelly 2/R.I.Rifles to hospital	
	7th		Battalion paraded at 12.40 p.m. and marched by Platoons to trenches in front of AUCHONVILLERS relieving 7th Bn. D.C.L.I. (Sheet 57 DSE 1/20,000 Sq 4d Central)	W.J.
Trenches at 1st Auteal.	8th		In trenches as above. Very quiet day. The enemy sent over a few 7.7cm shells and some minenwerfer bombs. Casualties Nil	J.

WAR DIARY
or
INTELLIGENCE SUMMARY

Army Form C. 2118

August 1916

Place	Date	Hour	Summary of Events and Information	Remarks and references to Appendices
Trenches at	9th		In trenches. Very quiet day. Enemy sent over a few Minn. Shells throughout the day. Our Artillery shelled the enemy lines throughout the day and no retaliation was forthcoming. Casualties 2 Other Ranks WOUNDED.	Map ref. Hébuterne Sheet 57D SE 1/20,000 and 57D 1/40,000
	10th		In trenches as above. Quiet day. Battalion relieved 7pm by 1st Grenadier Guards and marched to camp at BUS LES ARTOIS.	
	11th		In Camp at Bus.	
	12th		In Camp at Bus.	
	13th		In Camp at Bus. Following Officers joined the Bn. LT. G.C. ROBB } 3rd Bn. The Royal Irish Rifles. LT. N.V. POLLOCK }	

WAR DIARY or INTELLIGENCE SUMMARY

Army Form C. 2118

AUGUST 1916

Place	Date	Hour	Summary of Events and Information	Remarks and references to Appendices
BUS LES ARTOIS	14th		In Camp at BUS LES ARTOIS. Draft of 22 other ranks joined the battalion. The following men left the battalion to join the 36th West Division, having been sent to the battalion as a reinforcement by mistake. 35 men of 11th Bn. R. Inniskilling Fusiliers & men of 9th Bn. R. Inniskilling Fusiliers and 9 men of 10th Bn. R. Inniskilling Fusiliers.	Map reference Sheet 57D / 40,000 and 57D S.E. / 20,000
	15th		In Camp at BUS. Battalion paraded about 9.35 am and proceeded to a New Camp at ACHEUX. 2nd Lt H.D. SINCLAIR 5/R.I. Rifles to England sick.	Captain E.C. MALDEN RAMC joined the battalion in relief of Captain J.L. SULLIVAN RAMC who returned to field ambulance.
	16th		In Camp at ACHEUX.	
	17th		In Camp at ACHEUX. Captain W.B. TEELE 2nd Bn. The Royal Irish Rifles joined the battalion.	
	18th		In Camp at ACHEUX. The battalion paraded at 3.40 pm and marched to a New Camp at HEDAUVILLE. Draft of 15 other ranks joined the battalion.	
N. BLUFF 19th 57D S.E. 20,000 Sq. 36 Central E bank of R ANCRE	19th		In Camp at HEDAUVILLE. Battalion paraded at 2 pm and marched to dugouts at NORTHERN BLUFF (57DSE / 20,000 - Sq. 36 Central). Relieving 7th West Riding Regt. Relief complete 6.50 pm. The Battalion had to provide numerous carrying and working parties. Casualties Nil. D Company occupied strong points on W Bank of R ANCRE	
	20th		In dugouts at Northern Bluff. A lady morning following Casualties suffered by one other rank. 2/Lt. F.R. FOWLER 3/Seaforth Regt. wounded patio. * Remained at duty. Other ranks 3 wounded	

WAR DIARY or INTELLIGENCE SUMMARY

Army Form C. 2118

(Erase heading not required.)

Place	Date	Hour	Summary of Events and Information	Remarks and references to Appendices
NORTHERN BLUFF 57 D.S.E. 1/20,000 Sq. 36 Central	AUGUST 1916 20th (Cont.)		Quiet day. About 9pm – 10.30pm Enemy Shelled the BLUFF and the valley below with H.E. and Shrapnel. Small and large shells (4.7mm, 5.9cm) being used. Altogether 450 men were employed throughout the day and night on carrying and digging fatigues working parties.	
E. Bank of River ANCRE	21st		At the BLUFF. Quiet day. About 150 H.E. and Shrapnel (7.7cm + 5.9") fell in and around the valley of the ANCRE at the BLUFF. Small barrage fire done. The shells chiefly hitting the water. Throughout the night odd shells also came over. 450 men were employed in carrying and digging fatigues throughout the day and night. Casualties Nil.	
	22nd		At the BLUFF. Some shelling took place in and around the BLUFF. Usual fatigue parties were provided. Quiet day. Casualties Nil	
	23rd		At the BLUFF. Quiet day. Usual fatigue parties were furnished. Casualties 1 killed 3 wounded	
	24th		At the BLUFF. Quiet day, except for some shells falling near the battalion. Usual fatigue parties were furnished. Casualties 2 wounded	

WAR DIARY or INTELLIGENCE SUMMARY

Army Form C. 2118

Place	Date	Hour	Summary of Events and Information	Remarks and references to Appendices
NORTHERN BLUFF MAP 57 D. SE. 1/20,000 Sq 36 Central E. BANK of River ANCRE	25th		At the BLUFF. Quiet day except for usual amount of shelling. On the part of the enemy. Fatigue parties for working and carrying were furnished throughout the day and night (450 men) Casualties 1 Wounded. 2/LT. C.K. EDWARDS 5/Royal Irish Rifles to ENGLAND Sick	
	26th		At the BLUFF. Fatigue parties as above furnished by the battalion. The battalion was relieved by 1/WEST YORKS RGT. Relief complete 8 pm. The relief was delayed somewhat by the enemy shelling the valley of the ANCRE. The BATTALION marched to billets at BOUZINCOURT (W7) the last company arriving about 11 pm. During the day new trenches (about J x 3) were reconnoitred. Casualties 1 Wounded.	
	27th		In billets at BOUZINCOURT. Trenches about x 3 were reconnoitred during the day.	
	28th		In billets as above. The Battalion paraded at 4 am and marched via AVELUY (W17) to trenches R33c70 — X2 t-48 relieving 1/7 WARWICKSHIRE Rgt. Relief complete about 9.30 am	19

WAR DIARY or INTELLIGENCE SUMMARY

Army Form C. 2118

Place	Date	Hour	Summary of Events and Information	Remarks and references to Appendices
MAP 57 D S.E. Trenches X33C90 to X27 48	AUGUST 1916 28th		(Continued) Battalion headquarters occupied a trench where on 16.8.16 the battalion captured 2 officers and 126 other ranks (15 Rgt - PRUSSIAN) The day was quiet except for almost incessant shelling of the line by the enemy, particularly on the right four line. Units on Our flanks being - on the right ANZACS (4th Bde) and on the left 11th Lancashire Fusiliers. Connection was made with the ANZACS by means of patrols; the front line on the right being very weakly held with Lewis guns and small posts owing to the shelling. Trenches badly knocked about and hit. Casualties 1 killed 28 wounded	
	29th		A trenches as above. Quiet day except for heavy shelling from enemy on the front line. A patrol went out to establish a post at R32d 23 but owing to the ground being so very badly knocked about and trenches obliterated the objective could not be recognised or reached. It rained fairly heavily during the day and trenches were very wet. Casualties 5 wounded.	

WAR DIARY or INTELLIGENCE SUMMARY

Army Form C. 2118

Place	Date	Hour	Summary of Events and Information	Remarks and references to Appendices
MAP 57DSE 1/20,000 Trenches X33c70 to X2b48	AUGUST 1916			
	30th		9 Trenches. Quiet day except for enemy shelling our lines. Trench was maintained with the ANZACS. A patrol went out and reconnoitred enemy trenches. Trenches were heavy wet and rain fell throughout the day. 2/Lt T.J. DALY 32d Benata Regt. wounded. Other Ranks 5 killed 16 wounded	
	31st		9 Trenches as above. Enemy shelled our line throughout the day	

J Sharpe Lt Col
Comdg 1/K Amp R
31.8.16

74th. INFANTRY BDE.
25th. DIVISION

2nd. ROYAL IRISH RIFLES

SEPTEMBER 1916.

Vol 21
2/R.I.Rifles
22

Army Form C. 2118

WAR DIARY
or
INTELLIGENCE SUMMARY
(Erase heading not required.)

Instructions regarding War Diaries and Intelligence Summaries are contained in F.S. Regs., Part II. and the Staff Manual respectively. Title Pages will be prepared in manuscript.

Place	Date	Hour	Summary of Events and Information	Remarks and references to Appendices
Sheet 57D / 40,000 Sq X 3	1st		SEPTEMBER 1916. In trenches in front of OVILLERS. Relieved by 13th Cheshire Regiment. Relief complete about. A and C Companies occupied dugouts in OVILLERS and C and D Companies occupied dugouts at DONNETS POST (X) the battalion being in Bde Reserve. Working parties were found throughout the day and night working on the front line and communication trenches. Casualties 1 other Rank wounded Lieut J.R. TUCKETT to Field Ambulance sick. 6 other Ranks joined the battalion. Strength of Bn. 25 Officers 695 other Ranks.	X 2nd Bn. THE ROYAL IRISH RIFLES
Bde Reserve	2nd		In Brigade Reserve as above. Usual working parties found. Draft of 5 other ranks. Battle Casualties nil. 1 2/Lt F.P. CROWLEY 3rd Leinster Regt. to Field Ambulance. Quiet day.	
	3rd		In Brigade Reserve as above. Working parties found as above. Relieved by Lieut ANDREW BEACONSFIELD Captain STOTT R.A.M.C. 2nd Lt. MARTIN JOSEPH McDONNEL 2/R.I.Rifles ROSS R.A.M.C. joined the battalion, having received a Regular commission from the Irish Guards. Battle Casualties nil.	

Army Form C. 2118

WAR DIARY
or
INTELLIGENCE SUMMARY
(Erase heading not required.)

Instructions regarding War Diaries and Intelligence Summaries are contained in F.S. Regs., Part II. and the Staff Manual respectively. Title Pages will be prepared in manuscript.

Place	Date	Hour	Summary of Events and Information	Remarks and references to Appendices
			SEPTEMBER 1916	
Bde Reserve Sheet 57 D 1/40,000	4th		2 Bde Reserve. Usual working parties found. Quiet day. Battn Casualties 4 other ranks wounded.	
	5th		2 Bde Reserve as above. Issue working parties in front line and support found. Major Joseph JEROME SACCONE HASKETT-SMITH 2nd Royal Irish Rifles joined the battalion. Battn Casualties 1 other rank wounded. Draft of 37 other ranks joined the battalion.	
	6th		2 Bde Reserve as above. Battalion relieved by 6th BORDER REGT. Relief complete about 8 am. Battn Casualties Nil. Battalion marched in ?? parties to Camp at V 12 Central.	
ACHEUX	7th		2 Camp as above. Battalion moved to huts in ACHEUX Wood arriving there about 4.30 pm. 30 other ranks left the battalion to join their own units in the 36th Ulster Division having been posted to this battalion in error.	
	8th		2 Huts as above. Battalion paraded at 12 noon and was addressed by the G.O.C. 25th Division. At 12.45 pm it marched	

Army Form C. 2118

WAR DIARY
or
INTELLIGENCE SUMMARY
(Erase heading not required.)

Instructions regarding War Diaries and Intelligence Summaries are contained in F. S. Regs., Part II. and the Staff Manual respectively. Title Pages will be prepared in manuscript.

Place	Date	Hour	Summary of Events and Information SEPTEMBER 1916	Remarks and references to Appendices
PUCHEVILLERS	8th (contd)		off by Companies to PUCHEVILLERS arriving there about 3 p.m. and billeted	
Map LENS II 1/10,000	9th		2 billets as above. 5 officers went to AMIENS under Bde. arrangements.	
BEAUVAL	10th		In billets as above. Battalion paraded at 7 a.m. and marched to BEAUVAL and billeted	
BERNEUIL	11th		In billets as above. Battalion paraded 12.15 p.m. and marched by Companies at 300x to BERNEUIL arriving about 3 p.m.	
S.I.	12th		In billets as above. 2nd Lieut PAYNE Connaught Rangers and 2nd Lieut Daly Leinster Regt. rejoined the battalion from hospital. The battalion paraded at 8 a.m. and marched to billets at DOMQUEUR arriving there about 12 noon.	

WAR DIARY or INTELLIGENCE SUMMARY

Army Form C. 2118

Place	Date	Hour	Summary of Events and Information	Remarks and references to Appendices
DOMQUEUR Map LENS 11.	SEPTEMBER		1916.	
	13th		In billets at DOMQUEUR. The usual training programme was carried out. LT. WILLIAMS 5/Royal Irish Rifles joined the battalion. Draft of 18 other ranks joined the battalion.	
	14th		In billets as above. Training was carried out. LT. J.R. TUCKETT 2/Royal Irish Rifles rejoined the battalion from hospital.	
	15th		In billets as above. Usual training was carried out. LT. Colonel L.C. SPRAGUE 2/Royal Irish Rifles took over temporary command of 74th Infantry Brigade.	
	16th		In billets as above. Usual training was carried out.	
	17th		In billets as above. Battalion paraded at 2 p.m. and marched to a field 300x S of first O. in HOUDENCOURT and attended a lecture by Lt R. Stokes of 4th Army School on Drill & Guard	x

Army Form C. 2118

WAR DIARY
or
INTELLIGENCE SUMMARY
(Erase heading not required.)

Instructions regarding War Diaries and Intelligence Summaries are contained in F. S. Regs., Part II. and the Staff Manual respectively. Title Pages will be prepared in manuscript.

Summary of Events and Information SEPTEMBER 1916

Place	Date	Hour	Summary of Events and Information	Remarks and references to Appendices
Map LENS II. DOMQUEUR	17th		(cont) mounting etc.	
	18th		In billets at DOMQUEUR. Very hot day. Usual training was carried out.	
	19th		In billets as above. Very hot day. Training was carried out. 2ND LT. G.W. PAYNE 4th Connaught Rangers to Field Ambulance.	
	20th		In billets as above. Training was carried out.	
	21st		In billets as above. Training was carried out.	
	22ND		In billets as above. Training was carried out	
	23rd		In billets as above. Training was carried out. 2/LT. B.K. LOYD 2/R.I. Rifles to hospital sick.	

WAR DIARY or INTELLIGENCE SUMMARY

Army Form C. 2118

Place	Date	Hour	Summary of Events and Information	Remarks and references to Appendices
DOMQUEUR Map LENS II 1/100,000 BEAUVAL	24th		SEPTEMBER 1916	
			In billets at DOMQUEUR. Training was carried out	x
	25th		In billets as above. The battalion paraded at 6.45 am and marched in Brigade to BEAUVAL, passing the starting point (church at FRANCVILLE) at 8.20 am and arriving at BEAUVAL about 1 pm. The battalion occupied billets, but about 2 pm orders came to "Stand by". About 9.30 pm A. and B. Companies left in motor omnibuses to FORCEVILLE. The remaining two Companies left in motor omnibuses about midnight-arriving at FORCEVILLE about 2.45 am 26.9.16 when the battalion billetted	
FORCEVILLE	26th		In billets at FORCEVILLE. The battalion paraded about 2 pm and proceeded by Companies to HEDAUVILLE and billetted there	
HEDAUVILLE				
Sheet 57 DSE 1/20,000	27th		In billets at HEDAUVILLE. About 9.55 am the battalion paraded and marched by platoons to BOUZINCOURT, where it bivouacked in W8a. About 5.55 pm the battalion moved by platoons and relieved 8/WEST YORKSHIRE RGT. in the line from about W24 d 1.7 to R 19 C 1.1. The relief was somewhat delayed owing to faulty guides. Relief complete 3.30 am	

Army Form C. 2118

WAR DIARY
or
INTELLIGENCE SUMMARY
(Erase heading not required.)

Place	Date	Hour	Summary of Events and Information	Remarks and references to Appendices
Trenches Sheet 57 D S.E. 1/20,000	SEPTEMBER		1916	
	28th		In trenches W24 d.1.7 R19 C.11. Throughout the day the trenches were heavily shelled by enemy artillery except for very heavy trench shelling the day was uneventful. Patrols were sent out at night and information gained. Casualties 2/Lt. J.F. STEIN 3/Royal Irish Rifles KILLED. 2/Lt. K. ELPHICK 5/Royal Irish Rifles WOUNDED. Other Ranks Killed 3. Wounded Nil.	
	29th		In trenches as above. Heavy shelling throughout the day. Our line was extended to the East, the battalion taking over from 11/Lancashire Fusiliers to E. end of parallels to INNISKILLING Avenue (R19 C 16). Casualties 3 Killed. 14 Wounded.	
	30th		In trenches as above. Heavy shelling throughout the day and trenches badly knocked about. The battalion was being relieved by 7/A. W. Kent Regt. about 7 am when the relief was stopped. Two other companies had however appeared but the remaining two were stopped. The 7/A W. Kent Regt. into relieving our but with one Company. The Company remained as well. Heavy shelling throughout the day. Wounded (Other Ranks) (2 Coys) previous to ENGLEBELMER. Casualty 2/Lt. I. Ralph, Lees, 5 [illegible] 30.9.16	

74th Inf. Bde.

25th Division.

2nd Battn.

ROYAL IRISH RIFLES,

OCTOBER, 1916.

2nd R.I. Rifles.

WAR DIARY
or
INTELLIGENCE SUMMARY
(Erase heading not required.)

Army Form C. 2118
Vol 22

Place	Date	Hour	Summary of Events and Information OCTOBER 1916	Remarks and references to Appendices
Trenches and ENGLEBELMER Map Sheet 57^D / 20,000.	1st		Two Companies of the battalion at ENGLEBELMER. (i.e. C, ½D + ½B Coys) The remainder of the battalion was still in the line above THIEPVAL Wood. About R2h d 1.7 – R19 c 1.1 Throughout the day shelling was somewhat severe. Otherwise there was little to report. Casualties	
ENGLEBELMER	2nd		In trenches as above. About 5.30 a.m. the remainder of the battalion still in the line was relieved and joined the rest of the battalion at ENGLEBELMER. About 12.40 p.m. the battalion paraded and marched to Camp at W8 Central. Casualties	
Camp W8 Central	3rd		In Camp at W8 Central. A good deal of rain fell and it was very wet.	
	4th		In Camp as above. Very wet, which interfered with training.	

23

WAR DIARY
or
INTELLIGENCE SUMMARY.

Army Form C. 2118.

Place	Date	Hour	Summary of Events and Information	Remarks and references to Appendices
Camp W & Central Map sheet 57DSS	OCTOBER 1916 5th		In Camp at W & Central. Army huts. MAJOR W.J.T.S. HASKETT-SMITH 2nd S. Lancashire Regt. as acting Senior Major of that Regt. proceeded to join 2nd S. Lancashire Regt. Two Companies reported at AVELUY Siding for work at 8.30 a.m. being relieved in turn by the remaining two Companies after Battalion. The whole on completion of work went to OVILLERS POST	
OVILLERS POST.	6th		At OVILLERS POST. About 2 p.m. the battalion moved off by platoons and relieved 8th South Lancashire Regt. in Reserve. Two Companies being located in OVILLERS, one Company in MOUQUET Farm and one Company in a trench about R22c82. Relief complete about 5.30 p.m. Casualties NIL	
In Reserve	7th		In Reserve as above. Some shells fell in the vicinity of the two forward Companies. "B" Company was moved up from OVILLERS and occupies a trench near POZIERES Cemetery. The day was fairly wet. Casualties. 8. O Ranks W.I.A.	

WAR DIARY or INTELLIGENCE SUMMARY

Army Form C. 2118.

Place	Date	Hour	Summary of Events and Information	Remarks and references to Appendices
In Reserve B.H.Q. R28d14	OCTOBER 1916			
	8th	—	In Reserve. One Company MOUQUET FARM, 1 Company near POZIERES Cemetery, 1 Company in trench about R2c&2. The Fourth Company was moved up from OVILLERS and occupied a tunnel near MOUQUET FARM. Working parties were found throughout the day and night. Weather fairly wet. Shelling slight and generally uncentralized when parties were out working. Casualties 4 O.R. Wounded.	
	9th	—	In Reserve as above. Usual working parties were found by the battalion. Quiet day except for some shelling in the vicinity of companies and battalion headquarters. 2/Lt. C.R. COONEY 3rd Shields Regt. attached 2/Royal Irish Rifles killed in action. 5 O.R. wounded.	
	10th	—	In Reserve as above. Usual working parties found. Quiet day except for normal shelling as above. Weather fine. Casualties nil. 2/R.S.M. Murphy W.I.A. (at duty)	
	11th	—	In Reserve as above. Working parties found by the battalion as usual. Quiet day except for usual shelling. Casualties 1 wounded.	
	12th	—	In Reserve as above. Usual working parties found. Quiet day. Casualties 2 killed 1 wounded	

Army Form C. 2118.

WAR DIARY
or
INTELLIGENCE SUMMARY.
(Erase heading not required)

Instructions regarding War Diaries and Intelligence Summaries are contained in F. S. Regs., Part II. and the Staff Manual respectively. Title pages will be prepared in manuscript.

Place	Date	Hour	Summary of Events and Information OCTOBER 1916	Remarks and references to Appendices
In Reserve about R28 d 14	13th		In Reserve. The battalion relieved the 9th LOYAL NORTH LANCS Regt. in the front line from about R28 c to R22 d. Bn. H.Q. at R28 d 87. Lieut. T.R. TUCKETT 2/R.I Rifles Wounded. Relief complete about 7am. Quiet day except for desultory shelling throughout the day. Three Companies were in the front line and one in Reserve in ZOLLERN Trench about R28 b. Casualties O.R. Nil.	
Trenches	14th		In Trenches as above. Nothing much to report. The enemy shelled our front line occasionally throughout the day. The trenches were improved and a new trench commenced joining up the right of the battalion to the left of 55th Bde. on the night. Casualties 11 O. Ranks W.I.A.	
"	15th		In trenches as above. The usual amount of shelling took place. One Coy. being occupied in carrying during the night about R22. Work on improving the trenches was continued. Fine weather. Casualties O.R. 11 Wounded	I.C.S.

2353 Wt. W2544/1454 700,000 5/15 D.D.&L. A.D.S.S./Forms/C. 2118.

Army Form C. 2118.

WAR DIARY
or
INTELLIGENCE SUMMARY.
(Erase heading not required.)

Instructions regarding War Diaries and Intelligence Summaries are contained in F. S. Regs., Part II. and the Staff Manual respectively. Title pages will be prepared in manuscript.

Place	Date	Hour	Summary of Events and Information 1916	Remarks and references to Appendices
MAP Reference Sheet 57 DSE Trenches about R.22 c.d.	16th		In Trenches. Nothing unusual to report. Our artillery shelled the enemy line throughout the day. Work on the front line and Communication trenches was continued. Casualties Nil	
	17th		In Trenches. The day was rather wet, damaging the trenches to small extent. The usual work was carried on. Our artillery continued to shell the enemy line. Nothing unusual to report. Casualties 2 O.R. killed 1 O.R. W.IA.	
	18th		In Trenches. Wet weather. Usual shelling continued. The front line was slightly reorganised as an assault from our lines (HESSIAN trench) on to the German line (REGINA trench) was intended to take place on the morrow. In consequence the battalion extended to the west taking over about 200 x more of the line. 2/Lt F.R. FOWLER 3/Leinster Rgt. attached 2/R.I. Rifles was killed while reconnoitring the new post the line to be taken over. Casualties 3.R. 1 Introduced W.IA.	

2353 Wt. W2544/1454 700,000 5/15 D. D. & L. A.D.S.S./Forms/C. 2118.

WAR DIARY or INTELLIGENCE SUMMARY

Army Form C. 2118.

Place	Date	Hour	Summary of Events and Information	Remarks and references to Appendices
Trenches Map Reference Sheet 57D¼ /10,000 Grant R28 Oct	OCTOBER		1916	
	19th		In trenches. Bn. H.Q. moved to ZOLLERN trench about R28.b.37. The trenches here in a bad state owing to its wet. All efforts were concentrated in deepening and improving the front line ready for the intended attack on the morrow. Our artillery continued to cut the German wire in front. Enemy shelling was normal. Casualties 18 O.Rs Raids wounded (1 arrive D.O.W.)	
	20th		In trenches. Three companies in HESSIAN trench and one in ZOLLERN trench. Casualties 1 O.R. WIA 1 R.I.A 5 O.R. missing. Draft of 12 O.R. joined.	
	21st		The Battalion was relieved in HESSIAN trench during the early morning by the 11th Lancashire Fusiliers, 13th Cheshires, and 9th Loyal North Lancs preparatory to these battalions taking part in an attack against REGINA TRENCH. At 12.6 P.M. an intense artillery barrage was placed in front of REGINA TRENCH, and the three above mentioned battalions with a portion of the 53rd Inf. Brigade on our right, and of the 75th Inf. Brigade on our left attacked REGINA TRENCH. This battalion	

WAR DIARY or INTELLIGENCE SUMMARY

Army Form C. 2118.

Place	Date	Hour	Summary of Events and Information	Remarks and references to Appendices
	22nd		did not actually form part of the attacking army, its task being to re-occupy and hold HESSIAN trench and supply carrying parties to remainder of the brigade after the objective had been gained. Half A Coy & half B Coy ran ZOLLERN trench filled with HESSIAN trench and took up the original front led by half the brigade. The remaining companies moved up from the reserve trenches and proceeded with the work of emptying our trenches, ammunition, water, and consolidating material to RE Co. HSA trench, which had been successfully assaulted. The work was carried out in a satisfactory way inspite our heavy shell-fire in some parts near a place of from front to his trench gains. The Battalion also sent working parties for employing prisoners to Brigade HQ. Casualties 1 Officer W.I.A (2/Lt. S.A. Bell, 2nd Royal Irish Rifles) + 8. O.R. W.I.A.	
	23rd		2 trenches. (HESSIAN & ZOLLERN Trenches) Battalion was relieved between 11.30 a.m. & 4.0. P.M. by the 2/7 th Bn THE QUEENS (Royal West Surrey Regt) and marched via OVILLERS and ALBERT to W.27.a. (Map Ref: 57 D S.E) where it encamped. Casualties NIL. BN moved in motor omnibuses to HARPONVILLE arriving there at 12.0 noon. Bn billeted for the night.	
HQ in hut No 24. 67a			BN marched at 5.30 p.m. to BEAUVAL where it billeted	

Army Form C. 2118.

WAR DIARY
or
INTELLIGENCE SUMMARY.
(Erase heading not required.)

Instructions regarding War Diaries and Intelligence Summaries are contained in F.S. Regs., Part II. and the Staff Manual respectively. Title pages will be prepared in manuscript.

Place	Date	Hour	Summary of Events and Information	Remarks and references to Appendices
BEAUVAL	25th 26th		In billets at BEAUVAL. In billets at BEAUVAL. Gen Sir Douglas Haig & C.B. K.C.I.E. K.C.V.O. A.D.C. inspected the 74th Inf Bde and thanked individual commanding Officers for the front work of their respective Battalions had done during their operations on the SOMME.	
	27th		In billets at BEAUVAL. Capt Thompson appointed 4th Royal Irish Fus (attached) rejoined.	
	28th		In billets at Beauval. 2/Lt E.B.K. Loyd 2nd R.I. Rifles rejoined.	
	Sept 30th		In billets at Beauval. Capt Thomas 2nd R.I. Rifles rejoined. Lt McInerney At 10.30 A.M. 3rd Bn R.I. Rifles joined. Battalion headed to CANDAS station when it entrained for CAESTRE arriving there at 1.0 P.M. and marching to THIEUSHOUK.	
BN HQ at 31st Q.35.b.44 (coy HQ: B Service 27 D S.E.)			In billets at THIEUSHOUK.	

L.C. Sprague Lt Col
Cmdg 9th R.I. Rifles
3/. 10.76.

74th Inf. Bde.

25th Division.

2nd Battn.

ROYAL IRISH RIFLES,

NOVEMBER, 1916.

WAR DIARY or **INTELLIGENCE SUMMARY**

Army Form C. 2118.

W^n. The Royal Irish Rifles

SHEET. 1.   1916   Vol 23

Place	Date	Hour	Summary of Events and Information	Remarks and references to Appendices
THIEVSHOUK (near (CAESTRE)	1st	NOVEMBER	Battalion in billets. Battalion marched at 8.40 am to SHAEXHEN, near MERGREN, on N side. Arrived and billeted 10.30 am. 2/Lt MARRIOTT-WATSON joined.	Copy/6
SHAEXHEN	2nd		Battalion in billets marched at 8.30 am to Camp (Canvas and huts) on main road between BAILLEUL and NIEPPE, and 3 miles from NIEPPE. Arrived 10.30 am.	Cb/lr
	3rd		Battalion marched from camp at 12 noon to PLOEGSTEERT WOOD where they occupied positions in support of the 9th Royal North Lancs who were holding the front line. BN HQ at ERESLOW FARM, U.19. d.o.o (MAP REF: ST YVES, TRENCH MAP, 1:10000). The Battalion took over from the 20th Manchesters. Relief complete at 3.0 P.M. A Coy in Forts Everest, Dead Horse, and Boyd (Hunters Avr) B Coy in dugouts about PLUG STREET HALL (U.20.c.2.3.) C Coy in Forts Rupert, Eel Pie, Eccles, & Reading (in	Copy/1
BN. HQ. at 4 d.o.o 4	4th		HUNTER'S AV:) D Coy in TORONTO DUGOUTS and ROTTEN ROW (about U.15.C. central) Casualties NIL Battalion in support. Casualties NIL.	24/1 Copy/1

WAR DIARY of The Royal Irish Rifles

INTELLIGENCE SUMMARY

SHEET 2.

Army Form C. 2118.

Place	Date	Hour	Summary of Events and Information	Remarks and references to Appendices
			NOVEMBER 1916	
BN HQ at U.21.a.3.7	5th		Battalion in support. Casualties Nil. Draft of 8 other ranks joined.	C/A/p
	6th		Battalion in support. BN HQ moved further towards the front line to LEWISHAM LODGE at U.21. ECCLES, a.3.7. "C" Coy moved from Forts REGENT, EEL PIE, and READING, in HUNTER'S AV. to dugouts round GLOUCESTER HOUSE about U.20.c.5.9. (ST YVES 1:10000). CRESLOW FARM was taken over by 13th Cheshires, who also occupied the four forts vacated by "C" Coy. Casualties Nil.	C/A/p
ST YVES 1:10000	7th		Battalion relieved the 9th Loyal North Lancs in front line trenches from V.14.b.3.7. to U.21.b.3.5. (ST YVES 1:10000) Relief commenced at 7.0.am. and completed at 12.5 pm. BN HQ at HOPE HOUSE (V.14.d.8.1. ST YVES 1:10000). Casualties NIL. 2/Lt DAY struck off the strength of the Battalion.	C/A/p
	8th		Battalion in the line. Casualties Nil. 2.O.B. W.I.A.	
	9th		Battalion in the line. Casualties Nil. 2/Lt McDonnell returned from (sick) leave.	C/A/p
	10th		Battalion in the line. Gas discharge along Divisional front, commencing at 4.25 AM and lasting about 25 minutes, accompanied by a 3 minutes combined Artillery and Trench Mortars & Stokes Guns bombardment commencing at 4.30 AM. Apparently very little impression made on the enemy. ... Battalion relieved in the line by the 9th Loyal North Lancs, and took up the support positions. Relief commenced at 7.30 and completed at 11.30 AM. Casualties NIL.	C/A/p

Army Form C. 2118.

WAR DIARY
or
INTELLIGENCE SUMMARY

7/8 The Royal Irish Rifles

SHEET 3.

(Erase heading not required.)

Instructions regarding War Diaries and Intelligence Summaries are contained in F. S. Regs., Part II. and the Staff Manual respectively. Title pages will be prepared in manuscript.

Place	Date	Hour	Summary of Events and Information	Remarks and references to Appendices
			NOVEMBER 1916	
	11th		Battalion in Support. Gas discharged along Divisional front at 10 p.m. coupled with a combined artillery, Trench mortar, and Stokes gun, Three minutes bombardment 10.0 P.M — 10.12 P.M and 10.20 P.M — 10.22 P.M. Casualties NIL.	CB/jp
	12th		Battalion in Support. Casualties NIL.	CB/jp CB/jp
	13th		Battalion in Support. Orders issued as to new method of holding the line; 2 Coys Roy Irish Rifles to hold front line from U.15.a.0.5 (left of Brigade front) to U.15.b.3.0 (MAP: 5" Ypres 1:10000) with 2 Coys in support. The 9th L.N.L. to hold the line from U.15.b.3.0 to U.21.b.5.6 in a similar way. Casualties NIL. Draft of 11 Other Ranks joined.	CB/jp
HOPE HOUSE (U.14.d.8.1) Permanent	14th		Battalion in Trenches. 2 Coys in the line under new arrangement, 2 coys in support in ROTTEN ROW & St Andrew's Drive & Trench Dugouts. Permanent BN HQ in HOPE HOUSE. Move complete by 10.45 AM. Casualties NIL.	CB/jp
BN HQ	15th		Battalion in Trenches. Casualties 1 O.R. W.I.A.	OB/jp
	16th		Battalion in Trenches. Casualties NIL	CB/jp
	17th		Battalion in Trenches. Two coys in support (C&D) relieved two coys in the front line. Relief completed by 7.45 AM. Casualties 2 O.R. W.I.A.	CB/jp CB/jp
	18th		Battalion in trenches. Casualties 7 other ranks (draft) joined.	CB/jp

WAR DIARY 7B⁰ The Royal Irish Rifles
INTELLIGENCE SUMMARY

Army Form C. 2118.

SHEET 4

Place	Date	Hour	Summary of Events and Information	Remarks and references to Appendices
HOPE HOUSE. (U 14 d 8.1) (Map Ref. St YVES 1:10000)	NOVEMBER 1916			
	19th		Battalion in trenches. Casualties 2 O.R. killed. 3 O.R. wounded in action. Capt J Ferguson 8th R. Rifles joined Bn	C.H.R.
	20th		Battn — trenches. 2/Lt C.F. Wilkins 7/8 R Inn Fus. & Rifles rejoined from 25th Bns. Draft 6 O.R. joined	C.H.R.
	21st		2/Lt C. Sprosse Butler 8 Rifles handed over Command of the Battn. to Major J Emms & proceeded to England. Two Coys in Support A.H.B. relieved the two Coys in the front line.	O.H.R.
	22		Battalion in trenches. 2 O.R. W.I.A.	O.H.R. C.H.R.
	23		do	
	24		do	
	25		do Casualties 3 O.R. K.I.A. 1 O.R. W.I.A. Lieutenant Allen & Major H.R. Goodman joined Bn. O.H.R.	JHA
	26		Coy relieved each other in the line. A H.B. to Support from front line. Major H.R. Goodman 7/8 R. Irish R. Rifles took over Command of the Bn. from Major Emms.	JHA JHA
	27		Battn in trenches. Casualties 1 O.R. W.I.A. 1 in Draft 2.5 O.R. joined.	JHA
	28		do Major J Emms left the Battn on Command. Draft 7 O.R. joined	
	29		do Casualties 1 O.R. W.I.A.	
	30		do Coys relieved each other. A.H.B. to front line from Supports. 1 O.R. W.I.A.	
			do 2nd Lieut Peach rejoined from 7/8th B.Rs.	

J.R. Robinson Major.
Commdg 7/8th The Royal Irish Rifles.

74th Inf. Bde.

25th Division.

2nd Battn.

ROYAL IRISH RIFLES,

DECEMBER, 1916.

WAR DIARY or INTELLIGENCE SUMMARY.

Army Form C. 2118.

12th Bn The Royal Dublin Rifles

December 1916   Vol 24

Place	Date	Hour	Summary of Events and Information	Remarks and references to Appendices
HOPE	1st		Battn in trenches B+A Coys in front line C+D in supports Quadilhez 1 OR WIA	Map ST YVES 1:10000
HOUSE	2nd		— do —	
(Wud Ed)			French Bn (relieved) Capt G.S. NORMAN returned from Bn.	a guest there was a garrison late
Bulon Or.	3rd		Coys relieved each other in the line C+D to firing line, A+B to supports 3 OR reinforcements 1 OR KIA	
	4th		Battn in trenches 2/Lt W.R.N. Capt	
	5th		— do — Capt W. GRAHAM attached for instruction from ENGLAND 4 OR reinforcements	
	6th		— do —	
	7th			MS009
	8th		Coys relieved each other in the line A+B to firing line C+D to supports Rn Me BRIDE killed by sniper FG CMc 1 OR W1A
	9th		Battn in trenches Capt Graham left Battn 2 OR WIA	
			3/Lt P. A.D. JACKSON 2/Lt OR draft joined	
	10th		— do —	
	11th		— do —	
	12th		— do — Capt C.E. Barton Lt R.M. Kyllo and 31 OR draft joined 2 OR WIA	
	13th		Coys relieved each other in the line C+D to firing line A+B to supports 1 OR KIA	
			Battn in trenches	
	14th		— do — Relieved by 11th London the Battn marched to roots to REGINA CAMP	
			134 OR joined to draft (including 63 OR from 11/12 London Ref.)	

J.R. Brooke Lt Col

Army Form C. 2118.

WAR DIARY "7"B. The Kings. Rifle
or
INTELLIGENCE SUMMARY.
(Erase heading not required.)

Sheet 2   December 1916.

Place	Date	Hour	Summary of Events and Information	Remarks and references to Appendices
REGINA CAMP.	15		Battn in Huts. In Br on parade. Majority of Battn employed on & about the front line on working parties	July
	16		— do —	July
	17		— do —	July
	18		— do — Capt W.B. Stride and 16 to 4 Cheshire Regt for duty.	July
	19		— do — QMS joined Battn for duty	July
	20		— do —	July
	21		Bty Sergt on attachment to 25th Div School METEREN.	July
METEREN	22		Bn left Regina & went into Billets at Nippe.	M
	23		Fatigue front line	M
	24		Maj. Robins 3 Bn. joined for duty from home.	M
	25		Xmas day – Bn. shot – good dinner – Gen Bethel came over cheered them well.	M
	26		Fatigues front line	M
	27		4 O.Rs joined from Base – all belonging to RoyR. Fatigues front line	M
	28		Capt S.M Thomas to 4 Bde for attachment	"
	29		Capt Ferguson 5 Bn sent to Base as D.B.O. over age for front line.	"
	30		2 Col Ritchie joined Bn to go as 2 in command. Fatigues front line	"
	31		B coy reformed from "Metaren" under Capt Burton.	"

SECRET.

Copy No. 19

War Diary

74TH INFANTRY BRIGADE OPERATION ORDER NO. 97.

Map Reference.
Sheet 36 N.W. Edition 6
1/20.000.
1/20000 Trench Map issued
with Defence Scheme.

2nd December 1915.

1. The Brigade frontage will be from junction of new trench with old front line trench U.15.a.0.4 to junction of STRAND trench with U.21.6 inclusive. On our left the boundary between 25th Division and 36th Division will be the junction of the new trench at U.15.a.0.4 with the old front line trench to U.14.d. 25.65 - along tram line to HYDE PARK CORNER - thence along RED LODGE Road (inclusive to 36th Division) - to T.23.central - thence to G.H.Q. Second Line at T.22.a.5.8. ONTARIO AVENUE will be inclusive to 25th Division - AINSCROFT AVENUE and the tram line to 36th Division.
On our right between 74th Brigade and 75th Brigade the STRAND.

2. Reliefs as per attached tables.
All details will be arranged direct by O's.C. Units concerned.

3. TRENCH STORES.
All trench stores, grenades &c will be handed over on relief and receipts for same obtained. Gum Boots and Primus Stoves will be treated as the property of the Brigades and will not be handed over. Brigade Gum Boot Store No. 3 to 75th Brigade. Another Store No. 4 will be formed at the PIGGERIES.

4. ADVANCED PARTIES.
O's.C. 11th Lancashire Fusiliers and 9th Loyal North Lancs will send down advance parties to their billets tomorrow 3rd instant to arrive by 10.30 a.m. The advance party of 11th Lancashire Fusiliers will report at Brigade Headquarters at this hour. A Staff Officer will then take them round their billets in NIEPPE. Second in Commands, 1 N.C.O. and 4 men per Company. 1 N.C.O. and 4 men per Battalion Headquarters.
In the case of 9th Loyal North Lancs 1 Officer in addition will be detailed to take charge of Headquarter party.

5. ACKNOWLEDGE.

Captain.
Brigade Major.
74th Infantry Brigade.

Issued at
through Signals.

Copies to:
Nos. 1 & 2 to 25th Division.
3 to 11th Lancs. Fus:
4 " 13th Cheshires.
5 " 9th L.N.Lancs.
6 " 2nd R.I.Rifles.
7 " 74th M.G.Company.
8 " 74th T.M.Battery.
9 " 75th Brigade.
10 " 7th Brigade.
11 " 105th Field Coy. R.E.
12 " 6th South W.Bords.
13 " Brigade Major.
14 " Staff Captain.
15 " 199 Coy. A.S.C.

Copy No. 16 to 75th Fd. Ambulance.
"   "   17 " Brigade Signals.
"   "   18 " C.R.A.
"   "   19 " War Diary.

DATE.	UNIT.		FROM.	TO.	REMARKS.
	74th Inf. Bde.	75th Inf. Bde.			
4th Dec.	9th L.N.Lancs.	11th Cheshires.	Trenches.	GRANDE MUNQUE 2 Companies. PETITE MUNQUE 1 Coy & 2nd in command. REGINA Camp. Hdqrs. 1 Coy.	Companies at 200 yards interval.
4th Dec.	11th Lancs. Fus: (3 Coys in front line).	11th Cheshires.	Trenches.	2 Coys to NIEPPE KEEPERS HUT BAR- RICADE Company to PLOEGSTEERT HALL. Hdqrs remain CRESLOW FARM.	Companies at 200 yards interval.
5th Dec.	11th Lancs. Fus:	NIL.	PLOEGSTEERT HALL TOUQUET BERTHE, CRESLOW FARM.	NIEPPE.	Move not to commence before 10 a.m.
6th Dec.	N I L.	8th Borders.	HYDE PARK CORNER.	TOUQUET BERTHE. PLOEGSTEERT HALL & CRESLOW FARM.	

SECRET.

Copy No. 16.

71TH INFANTRY BRIGADE OPERATION ORDER NO. 98.

Reference Trench Map.   19th December 1916.
1/5,000 & 1/10,000.

1. A small wire cutting operation will be carried out along the whole Divisional front on Wednesday December 20th from 3.10 p.m. to 3.40 p.m.

2. The objectives of this Brigade will be:-

   (a) To cut a gap in the enemy wire about U.21.b.7.5 (junction of support and front line northern face of BIRDCAGE).

   (b) To catch and kill any enemy about in his trenches with short surprise bombardments of selected points.

   (c) To catch and destroy the personnel of the three located heavy Minenwerfers when they retaliate, with short bursts of artillery fire.

3. Artillery, Trench Mortars and Stokes Programme and allotment of Ammunition:-

   (a) Two 2" Trench Mortars bombard wire opposite objective from 3.10 p.m. to 3.40 p.m. Rate of fire 1 round per minute.

   Two 9.45 Trench Mortars will fire one round apiece at 3.10 p.m., 3.25 p.m., and 3.40 p.m. one Mortar engaging U.16.c.18.87 (No. 9) and the other U.22.a.05.50 (No. 16). Each Mortar will fire one round at above targets at 6 a.m. on 21st instant.

   (b) Four Stokes.- One Stokes will stop enemy front line from U.21.b.8.7 (junction of third BIRDCAGE line in the front line) northward.
   One Stokes - enemy front line from above point southwards.
   Two Stokes to enfilade BIRDCAGE third line from above point South-east.
   Rate of fire eight rounds per gun per minute.
   Times:-
       3.12 p.m.)
       3.30 p.m.) One minute bombardments.
       3.40 p.m.)
   Total number of rounds 96.

   Stokes Mortars bombardment will be repeated at 6 p.m. on the 20th for three minutes (96 rounds) and again at 6 a.m. on the 21st.

   Two 2" Trench Mortars will bombard at 6 p.m. on the 20th for five minutes, and at 6 a.m. on the 21st for five minutes, rate of fire one round per mortar per minute.

   Artillery.

   One 4.5 - two 18 pounders. Target - U.16.c.18.87 (No. 9).
   One 4.5 - two 18 pounders. Target - U.16.c.3.7   (No. 12).
   Two 4.5 - two 18 pounders. Target - U.22.a.05.50 (No. 16).

   One round per 18 pounder, four rounds per 4.5 Howitzer.
   Time - 3.15 p.m.

Artillery. (Contd).

Two 6" Howitzers in addition will probably be available to engage Nos. 9, 12, and 16, if they are active.

Artillery bombardment will be repeated at 6.5 p.m. on the 20th and 6.5 a.m. on the 21st.

Total expenditure of Ammunition.

Stokes.	288	rounds.
2" Trench Mortars.	80	"
Heavy T.M's.	8	"
18 pounders.	36	"
4.5 Hows.	48	"

4. Machine Guns.
   Two machine guns to enfilade enemy communication trenches East of BIRDCAGE concurrently with Stokes Mortar bombardments.

5. All Rifle Grenade Batteries will co-operate on suitable targets opposite their front during the 6 p.m. bombardment on the 20th and 6 a.m. bombardment on the 21st.

6. O.C. Sub-sectors will arrange to have their trenches clear of working parties and garrisons of trenches as much under cover as possible during the bombardments.

7. O.C. 13th Cheshires will endeavour to catch the enemy mending his wire during night 20th/21st with Lewis gun fire, and to ascertain with patrols extent of damage done.

8. Brigade Intelligence Officer will arrange for Brigade Observers to carefully watch the effects of each shoot, and endeavour to pick up correct bearings of any enemy heavy trench mortar that opens.

9. Signal time.
   Brigade Signalling Officer will send a watch showing correct time to all concerned between 11 a.m. and 1 p.m. on 20th December.

10. ACKNOWLEDGE.

J.C.Marriott Captain.
for Brigade Major.
74th Infantry Brigade.

Explained at 10.30 a.m. personally to O.C. Units concerned.

Issued at 8 p.m. through Signals.

Copies to:
1 & 2 Office copies.
3   25th Division.
4   11th Lancs. Fus:
5   13th Cheshires.
6   9th L.N.Lancs.
7   2nd R.I.Rifles.
8   74th M.G. Company.
9   74th T.M.Battery.
10   O.C. 2" Trench Mortars.
11   O.C. Heavy Trench Mortars.
12   O.C. Left Sub-Group R.A.
13   O.C. Centre Sub-Group R.A.
14   75th Inf. Brigade.
15   109th Inf. Brigade.
16   War Diary.
17   Brigade Signals.
18   **Brigade Intelligence Officer.**

SECRET.

Copy No. 16

74th INFANTRY BRIGADE OPERATION ORDER NO.99

Reference Trench Map.
1/50000 and 1/10000.   22nd December, 1916.

1. A small wire cutting operation will be carried out along the whole Divisional front on Saturday December 23rd from 11.45 a.m. to 12.15 p.m.

2. The objectives of this Brigade will be :-

   (a) To enlarge the gap in the enemy wire about U.21.b.75 (junction of support and front line North face of BIRDCAGE).
   To cut a gap in enemy wire at U.15.d.86.
   To smash in enemy trench.
   (b) To catch and kill any enemy about in his trenches with short surprise bombardments of selected points.
   (c) To catch and destroy the personnel of the two located heavy minnenwerfers (Numbers 9 and 12) when they retaliate, with short bursts of Artillery fire.

3. Artillery, Trench Mortars, and Stokes programme and allotment of ammunition :-
   (a) <u>Mortars</u> - Two 2" Trench Mortars bombard wire opposite U.21.b.75 from 11.45 a.m. to 12.15 p.m.   Rate of fire 1 round per minute.
   Two 9.45" Trench Mortars will bombard U.15.d.86 from 11.45 a.m. to 12.15 p.m.   Rate of fire 5 rounds per Mortar in 30 minutes.
   (b) <u>Stokes.</u> - One Stokes will step enemy line from U.15.d.86 southwards.
   One Stokes will step enemy line from U.15.d.86 northwards.
   One Stokes will enfilade BIRDCAGE third line.
   One Stokes will step enemy front line from U.21.b.87 (junction of third BIRDCAGE line with front line) southwards.
   Rate of fire 8 rounds per gun per minute.
   Times 11.45 a.m.)
   　　　 12 midday.) 2 minutes bombardments.
   　　　 12.15 p.m.)
   (c) <u>Artillery.</u> - 1 4.5" - 4 18 pdrs. Target U.16.c.18.87 (No.9).
   　　　　　 　" 　　" - 　" 　　" 　　　" 　U.16.c.3.7.   (No.12).
   　　　　　 　2 4.5" - 4 18 pdrs.   " U.22.a.05.50.(No.16).

   Two rounds per 18 pdr, Two rounds per 4.5 How each shoot.
   Times 11.55 a.m; 12.5 p.m.; 12.15 p.m.
   (d) <u>Machine Guns.</u> Two Machine Guns to enfilade enemy communication Trenches East of BIRDCAGE.
   One Machine Gun to enfilade enemy C.T. East of U.15.d.86 concurrently with Stokes Mortar bombardments.
   (e) 　　　All Rifle Grenade Batteries will co-operate on suitable targets opposite their front concurrently with Stokes Mortar bombardments.

   <u>Total expenditure of Ammunition.</u>

   　　　　　Stokes.　　　　　　192 rounds.
   　　　　　2" T.M's　　　　　 60   "
   　　　　　Heavy T.M's　　　　10   "
   　　　　　18 pounders　　　　72   "
   　　　　　4.5 Hows.　　　　 32   "

(2)

4. Os.C. Subsectors will arrange to have their trenches clear of working parties and garrisons of trenches as much under cover as possible during the bombardment.

5. 2" Trench Mortar will not register before 11 a.m.

6. Os.C 11th Lancashire Fusiliers and 9th Loyal North Lancs will endeavour to catch the enemy mending his wire and parapet during night 23rd/24th, and to ascertain with patrols extent of gaps made.

7. Brigade Intelligence Officer will arrange for Brigade Observers to carefully watch the effects of each shoot and endeavour to pick up correct bearings of any enemy heavy T.M. emplacements.

8. Brigade Signalling Officer will send a watch showing correct time to all concerned between 9 a.m. and 10 a.m. on December 23rd.

9. ACKNOWLEDGE.

                                                Captain,
                                        Brigade Major,
                                74th Infantry Brigade.

Explained at 12.30 p.m. personally to Os.C Units concerned.

Issued at 9.15 p.m. through Signals.

Copies to:-
1 & 2 Office copies.
3. 25th Division.
4. 11th Lancs. Fusiliers.
5. 13th Cheshires.
6. 8th Loyal North Lancs.
7. 2nd Royal Irish Rifles.
8. 74th M.Gun Company.
9. 74th T.M.Battery.
10. O.C. 2" Trench Mortars.
11. O.C. Heavy Trench Mortars.
12. O.C. Left Sub-Group R.A.
13. O.C. Centre-Group R.A.
14. 75th Inf. Bde.
15. 109th Inf. Bde.
16. War Diary.
17. Brigade Signals.
18. Brigade Intelligence Officer.

SECRET.

Copy No. 19

74th INFANTRY BRIGADE OPERATION ORDER NO.100.

Reference Trench Map.
1/50000 and 1/100000

27th December, 1916.

1. A small wire cutting operation will be carried out along the whole Divisional Front on Friday December 29th from 2 p.m. to 2.30 p.m.

2. The objectives of this Brigade will be:-

(a) To cut the wire about U.28.a.3½.8½. (on right of future Brigade front). For this operation 2" Trench Mortars, except one mortar have been placed at the disposal of G.O.C. 75th Infantry Brigade.

(b) To destroy heavy minenwerfers Nos:10 and 15 with Artillery, these having been now accurately located.

(c) To catch and destroy the personnel of 9 and 12 when they retaliate with 2 9.45" trench mortars and Artillery.

3. Artillery and Stokes programme and allotment of Ammunition:-

Artillery.

Two Batteries 18 pdrs; one battery 4.5 Hows., probably two 6" Hows.
Time of opening fire 2 p.m.
Targets and rate of fire to be decided by C.R.A. Loft Group.

Mortars.

Two 9.45" T.M's will engage Nos: 9 and 12 if the latter evince any activity.
Rate of fire 5 rounds per mortar in 30 minutes.
Duration of fire until enemy cease to retaliate.

2" T.M's.

One mortar will co-operate with Artillery against No.15.

Stokes.

Four Stokes will be prepared to stop the enemy front line, opposite the front held by the Brigade if any retaliation with small aerial torpedoes or Rifle Grenades takes place, otherwise they will not fire.
All Rifle Grenade Batteries will co-operate on suitable targets opposite their front, concurrently with the Stokes opening fire and not otherwise.

In conjunction with 75th Brigade bombardment 2 4.5 Hows will engage the 4 houses in WARNETON which overlook our trenches on ST YVES.

Ammunition available.

Stokes	320 rounds.
2" T.M's	30 "
Heavy T.M's	30 "
18 pounders	300 "
4.5 Hows.	200 "

- 2 -

4. O.C. Sub-sectors will arrange to have their trenches clear of working parties and garrisons of trenches as much under cover as possible during the bombardment.

5. The Brigade Intelligence Officer will himself in conjunction with Brigade observers carefully watch the effects of the shoot and endeavour to pick up correct bearings of any enemy heavy minenwerfer that may open.

6. Brigade Signal Officer will send a watch showing correct time to all concerned between 9 and 11 a.m. on December 29th.

7. ACKNOWLEDGE.

                                    Captain,
                               Brigade Major,
                             74th Infantry Brigade.

Issued at 10.15 p.m. through Signals.

Copies to:-
1 & 2. Office Copies.
3. 25th Division.
4. 11th Lancashire Fusiliers.
5. 13th Cheshires.
6. 9th Loyal North Lancs.
7. 2nd Royal Irish Rifles.
8. 74th Machine Gun Company.
9. 74th Trench Mortar Battery.
10. O.C. 2" Trench Mortars.
11. O.C. Heavy Trench Mortars.
12. O.C. Left Sub Group R.A.
13. O.C. Centre Group R.A.
14. 75th Infantry Brigade.
15. 169th Infantry Brigade.
16. War Diary.
17. Brigade Signals.
18. Brigade Intelligence Officer.

War Diary

Correction to 74th Infantry
Brigade Operation Order No. 100.
-:-:-:-:-:-:-:-:-:-:-:-:-:-:-:-:-:-:-

S E C R E T.

B.M.O. 161.

B.M.G. 387 dated 28th inst. is cancelled.

In accordance with Divisional Instructions Operation Order No. 100 is amended as follows :-

Artillery.

For 1 Bty. 4.5" Hows. read 6-4.5" Hows.

2" T.M's.

For 1 Mortar will co-operate with Artillery against No. 15 read:-

1 Mortar will cut gap in wire about U.15.a.3½.7½. If any other Mortar is available O.C. 2" T.M's. will cut enemy wire with it from any suitable position at same time and will report action taken to C.C. Sub-sector concerned.

Patrols.

C.C. Sub-sectors will endeavour to ascertain amount of damage done both by observation and by patrols.

ACKNOWLEDGE.

Issued at 11 a.m.

29/12/16.

Captain,
Brigade Major,
74th Infantry Brigade.

Issued to all recipients of Brigade Operation Order No. 100 dated 27/12/16.

Reference Trench Map.
1/5,000 and 1/10,000

SECRET.

Copy. No. 18

74th INFANTRY BRIGADE ORDER NO. 102.

30th December, 1916.

1. A small wire cutting operation will be carried out on the Brigade front on Monday January 1st 1917, from 10.30 a.m. to 11.15 a.m. The objectives will be:-
   1. To cut the enemy wire from U.15.d.8½.5. to U.15.d.8.6½.
   2. To destroy enemy front line U.15.d.9.4. to U.15.d.8.7. (these points are points of junction of communication trenches with front line).
   3. To destroy enemy minenwerfers Nos: 9 and 12 with Artillery.

2. Artillery, Mortar, and Stokes programme and allotment of ammunition.

   Artillery.
   Two Batteries 18 pdrs covering fire to 2" T.M's.
   One Battery 4.5" Hows target Nos: 9 and 12.
   One Battery 4.5 Hows target Nos:10 and 15, if these evince any activity after bombardment of 29th, otherwise all Howitzers will be concentrated on Nos: 9 and 12.
   Two guns will be ready to switch on to Nos:11 and 17 if those minenwerfers open.
   Rate of fire to be decided by C.R.A. Loft Group, who will also arrange for 4.2 Howitzer Battery located at U.18.a.80.15. U.18.c.6.9. on the 29th instant to be engaged should it open.

   Mortars.
   Two 9.45" T.M's will engage Nos: 9 and 12 if the latter evince any activity.
   Rate of fire 5 rounds per mortar in 30 minutes.
   Duration of fire until enemy ceases fire.
   In addition O.C. 9.45" T.M's will be on the look out for any heavy minenwerfer opening from a hitherto unlocated position, and if the latter is within his arc of fire he will engage same at once. Such a position is suspected about U.22.a.5.6.

   4 2" T.M's target enemy wire U.15.d.8½.5. to U.15.d.8.6½.
   Rate of fire one round per mortar per minute.

   Stokes.
   Four Stokes will be prepared to stop the enemy front line opposite the front held by the Brigade, if any retaliation with small aerial torpedoes or Rifle Grenades takes place, otherwise they will not fire.

   Ammunition available.
Stokes.	400	rounds.
2" T.M's.	180	"
Heavy T.M's	20	"
18 Pounders.	500	"
4.5 Hows.	500	"

- 2 -

3. O.C. Subsectors will arrange to have their trenches clear of working parties and garrisons of trenches as much under cover as possible during the bombardment.

4. Snipers will be on the lookout for any enemy exposing himself whilst watching the shoot from either flank of the bombarded portion. Fixed rifles will be laid on objectives on completion of shoot. O.C. Subsectors will ascertain by strong patrols the amount of damage done during night 1/2nd January, 1917 and will arrange for intermittent bursts of fire from Stokes Guns, Machine Guns and Lewis Rifles on the damaged portion of the enemy line, throughout the night.

5. The Brigade Intelligence will himself in conjunction with Brigade observers carefully watch the effects of the shoot and endeavour to pick up correct bearings of any enemy heavy minenwerfers or Artillery that may open.

6. Brigade Signal Officer will send a watch showing correct time to all concerned between 7 and 9 a.m. on January 1st 1917.

7. No reference to this operation will be made on any telephone. No registering will take place after 31st instant.

8. ACKNOWLEDGE.

                                                               Captain,
                                                            fr Brigade Major,
                                                      74th Infantry Brigade.

Explained verbally to
Os.C. 2" and 9.45" T.M's
and C.R.A. Left Group
at 11.30 a.m.

Issued at 2 p.m,
through Signals.

Copies to:-
1 & 2.   Office Copies.
3.   25th Division.
4.   11th Lancs. Fusiliers.
5.   13th Cheshires.
6.   9th Loyal North Lancs.
7.   2nd Royal Irish Rifles.
8.   74th Machine Gun Company.
9.   74th Trench Mortar Battery.
10.   O.C. 2" Trench Mortars.
11.   O.C. Heavy Trench Mortars.
12.   O.C. Left Sub Group R.A.
13.   O.C. Centre Group R.A.
14.   75th Infantry Brigade.
15.   109th Infantry Brigade.
16.   War Diary.
17.   Brigade Signals.
18.   Brigade Intelligence Officer.

Army Form C. 2118.

WAR DIARY
or
INTELLIGENCE SUMMARY

2 Bn. The Royal Irish Rifles

Vol 25

(Erase heading not required.)

January 1917

Instructions regarding War Diaries and Intelligence Summaries are contained in F.S. Regs., Part II. and the Staff Manual respectively. Title Pages will be prepared in manuscript.

Place	Date	Hour	Summary of Events and Information	Remarks and references to Appendices
Huts C.11.b	1st			
	2nd		Lt. Col. G. Baird Inspected the Bn. in parade. 8.0ʰ, Other 490.O.Rs. Highest Strength 2132. He intended every figure during the Inspection, looked fit & clean.	M)
	3rd			M)
	4th		Marched from Huts by Coys. took over Kemmel Phegstreet left subsector.	M)
	5th		Trenches — 2Lt Jackson K.I.A Line within approx. Wr lines	(M)
	6th		" —	(M)
	7th		Bn. in Support at Croulers Farm Phegstreet, relieved by 11 Inns. regt., Cheps Gun Bantry, persists M.E. nthrn to Lieut. within & Merriott Watson Batten in Support. 10R. W.I.A	(M) M) CDs
	8th		— do —	CDs
	9th		— do — 2nd P.M. FENTON from Royal Munster Fusiliers joined. R.Col. Smith joined from on leave U.K. 2Lt. R.B. Merriott Watson to 2R. 10R WIA	CDs
	10th		Batten relieved 11ᵗʰ Land Fus in the line. 2/Lt. R.B. Merriott Watson was 2Lt. Ross ... proceeded ... leave. 10R. WIA (SW) Capt. H. G. Oliver R.A.M.C joined.	CDs
	11th		Batten in the trenches Phegstreet left subsector. 10R WIA. 10R. MIA.	CDs
	12th		— do —	CDs
	13th		— do —	CDs
	1st		Batten relieved in line by 11ᵗʰ James Fus. Marched to Kemmel Huts at REGINA Camp	CDs

26/

WAR DIARY
for the Royal Irish Rifles
INTELLIGENCE SUMMARY

Army Form C. 2118.

SHEET 2.

Place	Date	Hour	Summary of Events and Information	Remarks and references to Appendices
REGINA CAMP	15		January 17. Bath & Clean Rifles. Training of Coys & Specialists continued.	C234
	16		— do —	C234
	17		— do —	C234
HOPE HOUSE	18.		Battn relieved 11th Gloucesters in the line (Ploegsteert L/A Sub sector). 3 Coys in front line & Coy in Support. Capt E C Barton to hospital	C231
	19		In the trenches. 3 OR WIA Capt. J.C.C. Thompson returned temporarily from Bde Commander. C234 on Right. U.K. Child & 4th U.K. Suffolk	C234
	20		— do — 4. OR WIA Lieut West McKerrow 2/Lts J S Ryan Lt. T. Hicks 2nd R. Munsters and Y Junior	C234
	21		— do — Lieut J.J Houlehan 2nd Connaught Rangers joined. The Huns became very active with his artillery and more especially TMs during the latter days of this tour	C234
	22		Relieved by 11th Lancs Bn. Battn moves into Support area in PLOEGSTEERT WOOD. Bn H.Q. at Gloster Farm. A Coy GLOSTER HOUSE. B Coy holding posts along HUNTERS AVENUE C Coy PLOEGSTEERT HALL D Coy. TOUQUET BERTHE with one platoon at KEEPERS HUT BARRICADE. At 1.15 pm the enemy commenced to bombard our line with artillery and T M's. About 4.30 pm the bombardment became intense and at about 5pm the S.O.S signal was sent up from right sub section. Re inforcements had been called for by O.C 13th Cheshire Regt (right sub sector) about 3.15pm but the Brigade did not think the situation critical enough for reinforcements to be sent up from the Reserve at that hour. The bombardment became intense about 4.30pm. About 5.15pm the enemy from TOUQUET BERTHE was relieved & reinforce KEEPERS HUT BARRICADE. At 5.15pm the enemy from PLOEGSTEERT HALL moved to reinforce the troops at on HUNTERS AVENUE. About 5.30pm the H.Q. Coy & two platoons 11th Cheshires that the enemy had entered his trenches S of St YVES AVENUE. We asked for reinforcements. A Coy from GLOSTER HOUSE was sent up to St ANDREWS DRIVE about 7.30 pm in —	C234

WAR DIARY or INTELLIGENCE SUMMARY

Army Form C. 2118.

2/Bn The Royal Irish Rifles

SHEET 3.

Place	Date	Hour	Summary of Events and Information	Remarks and references to Appendices
	January 1917			
	22 (con'd)		had been expected. About 8pm the 3 Coys which were sent up to reinforce were requisitioned to working parties to repair damage done to the trenches. A much work as possible was done during the night and the 3 Coys returned to their respective positions in support area at daylight. Casualties - 2/Lt W.J.Scruell and 2/Lt W.J.Scully W.I.A. 1 O.R. K.I.A. 10 O.R. D.O.W. 1 O.R. W.I.A. 1 B.C.R. Draft joined. (Col Goodman returned from leave)	ORs
	23		Draft joined Capt R.D. Murtagh, 2/Lt Roy, 2/Lt R.H. Jones, 120 OR draft	ORs
			Jones [struck through] C.O.M.S.	
			Battn in Support.	
	24		— do —	
	25		— do — 1 O.R. (S.I.W.)	
Jerpt House	26		Battn relieved McLernan Thom in the line. A portions D Coy on right A Centre B on left B - Support. 2 ORs wounded (S.I.W.) Capt L.E. Barton reported from hospital.	Copy
	27		Battn in trenches. Capt T.J.C.C. Thompson returned to Bn. 2/Lt Ferns Coy.	Copy
	28		— do —	
	29		— do — 1 O.R. (W.I.A.) 1 O.R. (K.I.A.) 1 O.R. (Accd wound) 2/Lt P.G.Moffat 3 ORs Rejoined	Copy
Regina	30		Battn relieved in line by 11/5 Lance fus and moved to REGINA CAMP	Copy
	31		Battn in huts at REGINA	Copy

J.R.Wishman Maj
Commdg 2nd Bn The Roy. Ir. Rifles

WAR DIARY / INTELLIGENCE SUMMARY

Army Form C. 2118.

War Diary — The Royal Irish Rifles

Vol 26

27

Place	Date	Hour	Summary of Events and Information	Remarks and references to Appendices
REGINA CAMP	1 February		Battn in billets. Lieut. P.M. Fenton to hospital. No. 9772 R.S.M. P. Murphy proceeded to Commission Cadet in the Royal Irish Rifles	CRIR/1
	2		Battn was relieved by 10th Cheshire Regt 74th Bde at REGINA CAMP and moved to ROMARIN CAMP — 74th Bde now in Reserve.	CRIR/1
ROMARIN	3		Battn in billets	CRIR/1
	4		— do —	
	5		Battn in billets. Training commenced — attack practice in training area near BAILLEUL. 2nd Lt W.L.P. Bolton joined 7th & 8th Batts. Gun in Camp. 1 Officer its destroyed CRIR	
	6		Battn in billets. Training continued. Capt R.O. Manwaring and C.F. Burton attached to CRIR	
	7		Battn in billets — training continued	
	8		— do —	
	9		Battn attack practice carried out on Training Area near BAILLEUL	
	10		Brigade Route March. A/Sergt F. Elliot awarded CROIX de GUERRE (DRO No 21424/12/2/17)	
	11		Battn. Training in billets. Capt R.T. Jeffares to DW Musketry School	CRIR
	12		— do — Major J. Rosborough returned from Div Mus. School	
	13		Battn. Brigade attack practice in training area near BAILLEUL	CRIR
	14		Battn training in billets. A few gas shells burst in the vicinity of the Camp with little effect and no casualties.	
	15		Battn training in billets. Bomb accident on firing field. No 9641 Sergt C. Reading & Lieut Cruickshanks injured. Lieut E. Wilkinson slightly injured. 2 Nos Mills & Bomb 6. — prematures explosion	

WAR DIARY of The Royal Irish Rifles

Army Form C. 2118.

INTELLIGENCE SUMMARY

Sheet 2

Place	Date	Hour	Summary of Events and Information	Remarks and references to Appendices
Romarin	16		Brigade Route March	CRIR
	17		Brigade Attack practice on training area near BAILLIEUL. 2Lieut T.C. WALLIS + 4 Connaughts 2Lieut M. McFERRAN 4th R.I. Rifles	ORDERS
	18		Church parades No 8391 Sgt W. RAINEY R.I. Rifles posted as Regt M.O. 33 OR formed a draft	ORDERS
	19		Brigade attack practice	AB 2232g Supp R.O. Hange to Hospital
	20		Brigade to relieved by Brigade of 1st NEW ZEALAND DIV. Battn moved by ROUTE	CRIR
			to COURTE CROIX 3½ mile SSE of FLETRE	
	21		Battn move by route to EBBLINGHEM	
	22		Battn move by route to TATINGHEM	CRIR
	23		Battn at Rest in Billets No 9627 Sgt H.C. MALLETT and C.S.Mjr W. DOBBIE	
			War History R.I. Rifles posted a Zeroth B.G. a/22474	
	24		Battn at Rest in Billets 17 OR joined as reinforcements.	CRIR
	25		Battn in Billets - training commenced.	
	26		Route march 2Lieut P. MURPHY to Bde Grenade Coy.	
	27		Brigade Route march. R.M. Millar Commanded Battn all officers and 34 WNCO. CRIR	
			attended lectures at 2nd Army Inf School Wisques. 2Lieut R.S. WALSH 5th Ry Munster Proj. Joined	
	28		Battn training - outpost duties by Capt T.J.C.C. THOMPSON to joined from 7th Bn -- CRIR	
			Grenade Coy. Fighting Strength of Battn Officers 22. OR. 696. S.J.V. O'BRIEN	

M.A. Murphy Lt Col
Commdg 7/8th The Roy. Ir. Rifles

WAR DIARY or INTELLIGENCE SUMMARY

2nd Bn. The Royal Irish Rifles
Volume 2, Part II, Sheet 1.
Ref Map 27A S.E. 1/20000

Army Form C.2118. No. R.A.308 Date 1.4.17

Vol. 27

Place	Date	Hour	Summary of Events and Information	Remarks and references to Appendices
TATTINGHEM	1st		Batn in Billets. Lieut N V Pollock Struck off Strength of 2nd Army 4/1757 1/2/17	CMS
	2nd		Batn at Musketry on Range. Lieut D.J. Healop 5th Roy Munster Fus. Joined.	CMS
	3		do	
	4		Batn in Billets	
	5		Batn training - (Onposts) Capt R.O. Manserogh rejoined from Hosp.	CMS
	6		do - Road March & attack practice	
	7		Training in billets	
	8		do	CMS
	9		Road March & attack practice	
	10		Brigade Scheme to do	
	11		Batn in Billets	
	12		Range practice - Musketry.	
	13.		Gas attack practice. Lieut. H MARSHALL 5th Roy I Rifles Lieut W.H. CALWELL 5th Roy Irish Rifles Lieut D.Mc MAHON 4th Roy Ir Rifles and Lt. O.P. Smyth per Army AG A/9+83 a/7/3/17	CMS
	14		Batn Training in billets Major J EVANS Struck off Strength	CMS
	15		field practice on Range	
	16		Brigade Musketry Competition (Winners- No 2 Coy 2nd R.I.R.) Capt E. Y. THOMAS Struck off Strength	CMS
	17		St Patrick's Day Sports etc.	
	18		Musketry on Range Lieut W.C. HILL M.C. attd 7th T.M.B Struck of Strength.	CMS
	19		Batn in Billets +	CMS

WAR DIARY or **INTELLIGENCE SUMMARY**
(Erase heading not required.)

Army Form C. 2118.

2nd Bn.
No. RA 305
ROYAL IRISH RIFLES.
Date 1.4.17

Volume 2   Bn. The Royal Irish Rifles

SHEET. 1.   Ref. Map. 27A SE 1/20000

Place	Date	Hour	Summary of Events and Information	Remarks and references to Appendices
	MARCH 1917			
TATINGHEM & STAPLE	20		Battn. moved by train to STAPLE arriving in billets about 2.30 pm. Major E.L. Roddy the CHESHIRE REGT. took on Strength of Bn. Auth. WS. M6.2.6.17 dt/23/2/17	CBAM
STAPLE to STRAZEELE	21		Battn. moved by Route to billets in STRAZEELE AREA	CBAM
	22		Battn. in billets. 2nd Lt. B.J. Murphy 5th Roy. Munster Fus. joined	
	23		Battn. moved by Route to NIEPPE. Capt. N.G. May. Will. the Cheshire Regt joined.	
To NIEPPE	24		Battn. in billets - Provided 1 Platoon as WORKING PARTY	CBAM
	25		Battn. in billets - Church Services - Transfer - Major J. Rosborough 3rd (Res) Battn. R.I. Rifles struck off strength Auth. 2nd Army A/2.3.227 8/3/17	CBAM
	26		Battn. in billets - 2nd Lt. B.K. Caul ordered to Report to INDIA OFFICE LONDON	
	27		Battn. furnished WORKING PARTIES in PLOEGSTEERT SECTOR	
To OOSTHOVE FARM	28		FARM B11d 6.7. Capt E.M. Thomas The Royal IRISH Rifles rejoined. and moved to OOSTHOVE	Ref Sheet SHEET 36 N.W CBAM
	29		Battn. furnished Working parties as above No 9096 C.Q.M.S/T. McALINDON 9Bn. the Roy. I. Rifle promoted to Commissioned Rank Auth AG A/2/3553 dt 25/3/17.	
	30		Battn. in billets - furnished Working parties Ploegsteert Sector 1 OR WIA.	
	31		— No —	

Battn. Fighting Strength O. 22 OR 702
"   Total Strength   36   915

J.R. Goodman Lieut Col
Commdg 2nd Bn The Roy. Ir. Rifles

Army Form C. 2118.

WAR DIARY
or
INTELLIGENCE SUMMARY

(Erase heading not required.)

VOLUME II
SHEET 1
April 1917

2Bn The Royal Irish Rifles 24/75 Vol 28

Place	Date	Hour	Summary of Events and Information	Remarks and references to Appendices
OOSTHOVE FARM.	1st		Battn in Billets.	CRN
	2nd		— do — Major E.L. RODDY. (2nd Cheshire Regt) proceeded to 2nd Mn Brigade.	CRN
Renin/p. SHEET 36 N.W.	3rd		— do — Working parties providing L.R.	
	4.		— do — do —	
	5.		— do — do —	
NOOTE BOOM.	6.		Battn moved by route to NOOTE BOOM. 10 O.R. drafts joined. A Coy on WORKING PARTY.	
Rd/M.P HAZEBROUCK 5A.	7		Battn in billets. B Coy on Working parties.	CRN
	8.		— do — C — do —	
	9.		— do — D — do — 7 O.R. drafts joined. Capt P.M. Thomas to 2nd Army Sch.	
	10.		10.R. proceeded to Battn per R.E. Battn in billets — Bde attack practice — 2Lieut E.B.R. LORD struck off Strength Nth 26th Bn CRN A11/5A d/16/4/17. Working parties furnished to Coys.	CRN
	11		Battn in billets. — Bde attack practice. 2 O.R. joined.	
	12.		— do — 6 O.R. drafts joined. C/H R.O. MANSERGH to 28th Aus Inf Bn.	WRS
	13.		Battn moved by route into the line taking over the Sector held by 8/4 Border Regt from U.1.a.8.2. to N.36.a.55.35. A and B Coys front line. C & D Coys Support. Bn in Groups.	CRN/WRS
R.I. SHEET 28 SW			ST. QUENTIN CABARET.	
TRENCH MAP.	14.		Battn in the line as above. 1 O.R. W.I.A. Capt. Lt.B. TEELE rejoined Battn. R.I.A.	CRN
	15		— do — 1 O.R. (accessioning inclined killed) 1 O.R. W.I.A.	
	16		— do — 6 M.G. Coys moved into front line A P.B. to Support. 1 O.R. K.I.A. 10 O.R. W.I.A.	CRN
	17		— do — Gunther Win.	
	18		— do — 1 O.R. K.I.A. 10 R.W.I.A. 10 O.R. accidentally wounded	CRN

WAR DIARY *1st Bn. The Royal Irish Rifles*

Army Form C. 2118

Volume II
Sheet 2
April 1917

INTELLIGENCE SUMMARY
(Erase heading not required.)

Place	Date	Hour	Summary of Events and Information	Remarks and references to Appendices
ST VENANT CABARET	19		SHEET 28 S.W. Recce patrols. Battn relieved by 9th Loyal North Lancs in the front line & moved to ALDERSHOT CAMP 72 a 2.2. Enemy patrols encountered. 10R KIA 10R WIA 10R MISSING.	Cpt K
ALDERSHOT CAMP	20		Battn in billets. Bathing parties, foot inspection. 2O.R. left Battn & Capt W B TEELE & 25 (?)	OP K
	21		do — do — Lieut W.C. HILL attached 74th Div. 2nd Div. A.C. 378	Cpt K
	22		— do — — do —	Cpt K
	23		— do — — do —	
	24		— do — — do —	
	25		— do — — do —	Cpt K
	26		— do — — do —	
	27		— do — — do —	2 O.R. (attd 74th Tn (B)) K.I.A. Cpt K
	28		— do — — do —	Cpt K
	29		— do — 9 O.R. Army joined	Cpt K
NOOTE BOOM	30		Battn moved by route to NOOTE BOOM (via) area to ad were relieved in Reserve billets of ALDERSHOT CAMP by AUCKLAND Inft Regt N.Z.F. Fighting Strength 28 Offs. 823 O.R. Total " 36 " 941 O.R.	

J.R. Oldham
Lieut Col
Commdg. 1st Bn Royal Ir. Rifles

WAR DIARY
2Bn The Royal Irish Rifles B/6
or
INTELLIGENCE SUMMARY

Army Form C. 2118.

Volume 1. SHEET 1.

May. 1917.

Place	Date	Hour	Summary of Events and Information	Remarks and references to Appendices
NOOTE BOOM (SYNDICLES)	1st		Rd. Map. HAZEBROUCK 5A Battn in Billets. 7/Capt R.S.H. NOBLE 3/Royal Irish R/les joined.	
	2		— do — 6 O.R. amt. joined.	
	3		— do — Traing carried out — attack practice	
	4		— do — — do —	
	5		— do — Traing in hills	
	6		— do — Working parties furnished.	
	7		— do — Training Carried out — Rifle Attack Practice	
			Lt. J.V. Morgan the R.I. Rifles Lt. F. Brown 18. R. I. Rifles	
			2Lt. F. Moran 3rd R. I. Rifles joined	
	8		— do — Major H.T.T. Fish 3rd Worcester Regt left Bn. Capt. J. F. Zumeau	
			attached to Battn from Army	
	9			
			Training carried out	
	10		Battn moved from Pleurisy to Renin Eglise. Battn in Bivouac's relieving the	
			2nd Auckland by Regt N.Z. ? Capt E.M Thomas Struck off strength	30
			GHQ A/24650 6/5/14	
Renin Eglise	11		Battn in Support Working Parties furnished	
	12		— do — — do —	

WAR DIARY or INTELLIGENCE SUMMARY

Army Form C. 2118.

2nd Bn The Royal Irish Rifles

Volume 1. Sheet II

May 1917

Place	Date	Hour	Summary of Events and Information	Remarks and references to Appendices
Neuve Eglise	13th		Battn in Support. Working Parties furnished	2 O.R. W.I.A.
	14th		— do — — do —	Battn moved from Bivouacs
	15		— do — — do —	at 7.10. 8.21 to Village
	16		Battn relieved the N.Cd [Lancashires] Fusiliers in the line C&D Coys in the front line	
			C & A Coys in support.) 1 O.R. W.I.A.	
	17		Battn in Line. 1 O.R. K.I.A. 1 O.R. missing (believed killed) 3 O.R. W.I.A.	
			1 O.R. K.I.A. 2 O.R. missing 1 O.R. Shellshock	
			— do — C. Coy relieved "A" Coy in the line	
	18		— do — by the 9th L.N.Lancs in the line	Machine & Bivouac Camps
Bulford Camp	19.		Battn relieved at J 26 A.3.9. Working Parties furnished.	
J.26.A.3.9			Divine Service. Working Parties furnished. 5 L7 fighting	
Ploeg. Sheet 28 S.W.	20.		Battn in Reserve. Assisted from Rest Camps.	
	21.		— do — Working Parties furnished.	Lieut. J.G.MASSEY 2nd NZ.R.B.
	22nd		[Battn moved forth to ?] to enemy trenches	attached — Scout Read carried out inter Lieut McCalindon

WAR DIARY or INTELLIGENCE SUMMARY

Army Form C. 2118.

9th Bn. The Royal Ir. Rifles

May 1917

VOLUME I SHEET III

Place	Date	Hour	Summary of Events and Information	Remarks and references to Appendices
BULFORD CAMP	21 22 23		and that Walsh with object of parade to secure identification and prisoners. Coys. of Right and Centre Cos. in attack. Battn in reserve working parties furnished. — do — A friend entry rifle transport tapes representing by Rd. barbed wire, Hd. balistic infantry obstacle possibly to seem identification and prisoners. Operation orders attached. Appendix	
	24		Battn was relieved by 10th Cheshire Regt and moved to Camp and huttments near RAVELSBERG S16.d Ref map BAILLEUL 1/10000	
	25		Battn moved by route to Bailleul with transport thence by rail to WATTEN proceeding hence by route to TOURNEHEM.	
	26		Battn in Billets attack practice carried out	
	27		— do —	
	28		— do —	
	29		Battn moved by route to WATTEN and entrained morning by rail to Bailleul and thence by billets at La CRECHE. 2/Lt T.M. Gray & 5th R.I. Rifles joined	

VOLUME I
SHEET IV

WAR DIARY 2nd Bn. The Royal Irish Rifles — Army Form C. 2118.
or
INTELLIGENCE SUMMARY. May 1917

(Erase heading not required.)

Place	Date	Hour	Summary of Events and Information	Remarks and references to Appendices
LA CRECHE	30		Batt'n in Billets. Training carried out in vicinity. B'Ville.	
	31		do — do — 2nd R.D. Alexander 2nd R. Irish (joined)	

W.R. Goodman Lieut Col.
Commanding 2nd Batt'n The Royal Irish Rifles

WAR DIARY or INTELLIGENCE SUMMARY

Volume II 2nd Batt. The Royal Irish Rifles Army Form C. 2118.
Sheet I   June 1917   74/75

Place	Date	Hour	Summary of Events and Information	Remarks and references to Appendices
LA CRECHE	1st		Battalion activities. Training carried out.	
	2nd		do	
	3		do	
	4		do	
	5		Batt. marched from La Creche to Buzerines	
BUZERINES	6	1 P.M.	Batt. to Buzerines. 2 Platoons to lay wire over Battalion frontage of front	
			5th Brigade	
			Officers & O.R's then taken	
		3.50 P.M.	Batt. moved into trenches by the WESTHOF - NEWE EGLISE - WULVERGHEM Road	
		9.30 P.M.	Companies moved into Assembly trenches. "D" C & D Coys in Support trenches.	
			A Coy in Brigade Trench. At about 11 P.M. Battalion were in position.	
			The approach march was carried out in accordance with the plan of	
			Brigade operation order.	
			Enemy was shelling approaches in the vicinity of WULVERGHEM with the view to	
			preventing us to pass up. This caused a few casualties. However the	
			arrival was accomplished with very but slight incident. The Batt.	
			suffered few casualties during the time it was in position	

Volume I
SHEET III

WAR DIARY 2nd Battn The Royal Irish Rifles **Army Form C. 2118.**
or
INTELLIGENCE SUMMARY
(Erase heading not required.)

June 1917

Place	Date	Hour	Summary of Events and Information	Remarks and references to Appendices
	June 7th		Continued:— to darkness the officers of the carriage kept severe at 3rd + 4th the following moved forward through & consolidated from SLUG?? and AVENUE. It was known that the 9th R.I. Rifles were meeting with a stubborn resistance at MIDDLE FARM. In order in arrangement this position "B" Coy 2nd Battn the Royal Irish Rifles under Capt T. J. C. THOMPSON immediately pushed forward so to work round the FARM on the right flank and attack the FARM from his rear. Owing to the gallantry of OC "B" Coy the operations was entirely successful and the enemy now known at the FARM was roughly 60 killed. Further the more was recognition to occur support of advance without difficulty and work in conjunction with the 9th R.I. Rifles.	
	8	W=20 Officers? Wearing? 5 Machine Guns 2 Trench Mortars ammunition? Stores? KMR? Kennedy 15th Royal Irish Rifles? R.Irish? Casualties O/ As N/O Briens 15th Royal Irish Rifles 2/Lt D Fair 2nd R.Rifles Killed in action: Capt J/OC Thompson 2nd R Irish Fusiliers, Lt R.I.H. Neale 3rd R.Rifles 2/Lt W.C. Hewlett 2nd R Irish Fus., Lt H Murchison 5th R Irish Rifles, Lt F.L. Williams WIA: 11 O'Rourke (R/A 7th WIA (Shelby)) 2nd R.Rifles WIA K/A 209 ORs WIA 7 OR WIA (Shelby) 110R ORs killed 9 Missing (LRR since 1917)	

Volume I

WAR DIARY
or
INTELLIGENCE SUMMARY
(Erase heading not required.)

Army Form C. 2118.

3rd Batn The Royal Irish Rifles

Month: Nov 1917

Place	Date	Hour	Summary of Events and Information	Remarks and references to Appendices
	4th		Continued.- At 3.0 am. The Battn pushed forward in accordance with the plan of attack and by 5.0 am. the front line (A Coy) reached & attached to the attack and quickly closed up were found. When Bn HQrs Waterloo the front line the same follows started on the Canadian front line meeting little opposition. Wine had been exploded under Ontario Farm at 3.00 which apparently shattered the enemy's S.P. there. We were followed up the barrage which was so perfect to cause he each position when in a Linear manner with the advance a little persisting. The first objective was reached and within by the schedule hour. Consolidation of the lines although was commenced. The task was a difficult one as the enemy lines were almost obliterated. The 9th W. Lancs pushed through the Battn & in this way became 8 to Wilhelm up to the time of taking the final objective was in sight - the only difficulty experienced during the first hour of the attack was the indiscriminate protection - this was due to two things	

WAR DIARY or INTELLIGENCE SUMMARY

Army Form C. 2118.

2 Batt: The Royal 1st Fusrs

Volume I Sheet No 2

June 1917

Place	Date	Hour	Summary of Events and Information	Remarks and references to Appendices
	8th		Nothing of event happened during the day but work on consolidation was continued. The enemy artillery showed increased activity especially during the later part of the day, but no casualties I think were suffered in the sector occupied by the Battalion. Casualties 2/Lt Ogbourne WIA (at duty)	
	9		2nd Lt WIA Been in line consolidating captured positions. Working parties furnishing Casualties 2/Lt G.B. Rooke WIA	
	10		Battn in line 4 ORs major to the Royal 1st Fusrs WIA (two of whom 1/6/17) 5 ORs WIA	
	11		Battn withdrawn from line & Bivouacs at J.1+2. B Bivouacs returned	
	12th		Battn moved into Support Trenches in support of 15th Brigade 2 R WIA	
	13		1 OR WIA 6 Subalterns 2 OR WIA 1 PR Geo W	
	14		Battn relieved by the 7th Loyal North Lancs in Support line at 12 MN & the relief was completed at	

WAR DIARY

VOLUME II — 2/7th The Royal Irish Rifles

Army Form C. 2118

INTELLIGENCE SUMMARY
SHEET 3

Place	Date	Hour	Summary of Events and Information	Remarks and references to Appendices
SHEET 28 7.1.12.	15th		Battn in Camp	Ref Map trythcock 5-D
	16th		— do —	
	17th		Battn relieved 8th S. Lancs in the front line W of WARNETON A,C, & D Coys in front line. B Coy in Support. Capt R de L. Rose (5th Battn Roy. Ir. Rifles) joined — Major J. F. LEMAN posted to 11th Lancers In trenches as above. Casualties Revd. S. MERCER. W.I.A. Read	
	18th		W. H. CALWELL. W.I.A. O.R. 4 KIA 1 DoW 7 WIA In trenches. Casualties 2 O.R. WIA	
	19th		Relieved in the fire by 13th Cheshire and moved into support TRENCHES S.E. MESSINES. Casualties 2 O.R. KIA 3 O.R. WIA 10 O.R. draft joined	
	20th		Battn in Support — Casualties Nil	
	21st		Relieved by 43rd Bn A.I.F. & moved to Transport Lines in WULVERGHEM. NEUVE EGLISE Road. Casualties KIA = 2, DoW = 1, WIA = 3	
	22nd		Battn moved by bus to CAUDESCURE at 3 am	
	24th		Battn moved by Route to MOLINGHEM at 10pm	

Army Form C. 2118.

WAR DIARY
or
INTELLIGENCE SUMMARY

VOLUME II 17th The King's (L) Rifles

June 1917.

SHEET 4

(Erase heading not required.)

Instructions regarding War Diaries and Intelligence Summaries are contained in F. S. Regs., Part II and the Staff Manual respectively. Title Pages will be prepared in manuscript.

Place	Date	Hour	Summary of Events and Information	Remarks and references to Appendices
			Ref/Map HAZEBROUCK 5.A.	
FRUGES.	25th		Battn moved by route to ESTREE-BLANCHE	13/2b
	26		do — FRUGES. 2nd Lieut L.S. Ricks rejoined.	
	27		Battn in billets at FRUGES. 2nd Lieut G.F.F.V transferred to R.F.Corps.	13/2b/N
	28		37 OR staft joined. Training commenced 11 OR diet joined.	
	29		— do — continued	
	30.		— do —	

30/6/17

R.P. Roosebakl
Commanding 17th The King's L. Rifles

SECRET.

OPERATION ORDER No.38
- by -
LIEUT-COL. H.R. GOODMAN, COMMANDING, 2nd BATTN. THE ROYAL IRISH RIFLES.

Reference SHEET 28 S.W. 2 & 4,
Edition 4A, WYTSCHAETE and MESSINES,
1/10,000 and MAP "A", 1/5,000 attached.　　　　　　　　　June, 3rd, 1917.

---

1. INTENTION.　　　The 25th DIVISION will on ZERO Day capture the enemy system opposite it's Sector up to a line North and South through DESPAGNE FME: The New Zealand Division will attack on the Right of the 25th DIVISION and the 36th (ULSTER) Division on it's Left. The 4th Australian Divn: will then capture the enemy's system on the 25th DIVISIONS and NEW ZEALANDS Front up to a GREEN line inclusive (ODIOUS, ODD and OWL TRENCHES).

The 74th Brigade on the Right will capture the enemy First and Second Lines of Defence. The 7th Brigade on the Left will capture enemy first and second lines of defence. The 75th Brigade will then pass through and capture enemy third system. The 2nd ROYAL IRISH RIFLES on the Right and the 13th CHESHIRE Regiment on the Left will lead the attack of the Brigade. The Dividing Line between the 2nd ROYAL IRISH RIFLES and the 13th Cheshire Regiment is shewn by the centre dotted line on MAP "A".

2. OBJECTIVES.　　　The Battalion's Objectives are as follows:-
　　　(a). UGLY TRENCH.
　　　(b). UGLY SWITCH.
　　　(c). UGLY SUPPORT.
　　　(d). UGLY RESERVE.
　　　(e). UGLY LANE.
　　　(f). RIVER STEENEBEEKE.

Companies Objectives and Consolidation Tasks are shewn on attached Table (Appendix "1").

On the Battalion gaining it's furthermost Objectives, (i.e. S.P. in OZONE ALLEY and RIVER STEENEBEEKE) the 9th Loyal North Lancs: will pass through the Battalion and take their Objectives:-
　　　(a). STEENEBEEKE TRENCH.
　　　(b). OCCUR TRENCH.
　　　(c). INTERMEDIATE TRENCH.
　　　(d). OCTOBER TRENCH.
　　　(e). OCTOBER SUPPORT.
　　　(f). OZONE ALLEY.

3. INFANTRY ACTION:　　　The Battalion will move up to BRENEKERSCHEM between 9 a.m. and 11 a.m. and bivouac there 1 night. On the following Day the Battalion will parade at 6 p.m. and move down and assemble in jumping off trench in the following order:- H.Q. UNIT, "D" COMPANY, "C" COMPANY, "B" COMPANY, "A" COMPANY. Assembly to be complete by 11 p.m.

Route to WULVERGHEM in RED on MAP 1A (copy issued to O.C.Companies).

From WULVERGHEM to entrance of SNIPE AVENUE, route runs North of SOUVENIR FME: and is indicated by a line of WHITE flags, thence down SNIPE AVENUE and STONE STREET. The Battalion will move in a continuous stream in single file with no interval. Absolute silence to be maintained. No smoking after arrival at SNIPE AVENUE.

Assembly Trenches are allotted and will be occupied as follows:-

"A" COMPANY - LANCASHIRE TRENCH, covering the Left half of "B" COMPANY and the Right half of "C" COMPANY.
Flanks of Companies in assembly trenches will be indicated:
"A" Company - 2 WHITE Flags; "B" Company - 2 YELLOW Flags; "C" Company - 2 BLUE Flags; "D" Company - 2 RED Flags.
Boundary between the Battalion and 13th Cheshire Regiment is indicated by GREEN board.

4. **COMPASS BEARINGS.**
i. From Left of Battalion's Assembly Trench to Left of Objective UGLY TRENCH, 67 degrees (true).
ii. From Centre of Assembly Trench to Centre of Objective UGLY TRENCH, 60 degrees (true).
iii. From Right of Assembly Trench to Right of Objective (ONTARIO FME:) 47 degrees (true).
iv. From Left of Assembly Trench to SLOPING ROOF FMS:, 63 degrees.
v. From Right of Assembly Trench to SLOPING ROOF FARM, 46 degrees.

Officers concerned will set their compasses on these bearings, in accordance with the variation of their respective compasses.

5. **ATTACK.**
(a). At ZERO all Companies will fix swords.
(b). "B" Company will advance in lines of Platoon - Sections in file - 20 yards interval between Sections - 30 yards distance between Platoons. Nos. 1 and 3 Sections of each Platoon will advance to the Southern flank of OZONE ALLEY. Nos. 2 and 4 Sections of each Platoon to the Northern Flank. The 2 leading Platoons will envelope and mop up vicinity of ONTARIO FME: The 3rd Platoon will advance above ground along either flank of OZONE ALLEY as far as S.P., O.31.d.25.30. closely following creeping barrage. On completion of mopping up at ONTARIO FME: 1 Bombing Section and 1 Rifle Section will work along OZONE ALLEY and mop up. 1 Rifle Section and 1 Bombing Section will mop up all ground 100 yards South of OZONE ALLEY. Remaining 2 Rifle Sections and 2 Lewis Gun Sections will advance above ground along both flanks of OZONE ALLEY, pass through Platoon at S.P. O.31.d.25.30 to Junction of OZONE ALLEY and OYSTER TRENCH.
(c). "B" Company's Consolidation Task - Siting and digging, a C.T., from O.31.d.30.30 (Junction of OZONE ALLEY and OYSTER TRENCH), to O.32.a.15.00. (just North of SLOPING ROOF FME:)
(d). "C" and "D" Companies will advance simultaneously in 3 waves - leading waves objective, UGLY SUPPORT. 1 Platoon will temporarily remain in UGLY TRENCH to mop up any Dugouts that may possibly still in UGLY TRENCH and UGLY SWITCH. 2nd Waves Objective, that portion of THE OVAL in Battalion's frontage, and UGLY RESERVE. 3rd Waves Objective, UGLY LANE. Each wave will consist of one complete Platoon per Company. Care must be taken to maintain direction, and Platoons of "D" Coy. must do a rapid right incline and move quickly at first to close on creeping barrage.
(e). "A" Company will leap-frog over "C" and "D" Companies in two waves. Objectives S.P. and Dugouts about OZONE S.P., O.31.d.25.30. Leading wave 1 Platoon 30 yards in rear of "C" and "D" Companies 3rd Wave, followed by remaining 2 Platoons at 30 yards distance. On gaining Objectives, 1 Platoon will advance to the STEENBEEKE, will clear Battalion's Sector of all wire, and will render it passable for Infantry. Remaining 2 Platoons will construct a S.P. about OZONE S.P., O.31.d.25.30.
At ZERO plus 50, "C" and "D" Companies, Lewis Gun Sections of "A" and "B" Companies, will form up in Artillery Formation on the Eastern side of the STEENBEEKE, will advance and take over INTERMEDIATE TRENCH from the 9th Loyal North Lancs. "A" and "B" Companies, less their Lewis Gun Sections, will continue their consolidation tasks.

6. CARRYING PARTIES.

Each Company will have two Carrier Gangs. Each Gang will consist of 1 N.C.O. and 11 men. Badges 4" wide will be worn by these Parties on the Right arm:-

"A" COY. ... WHITE.
"B" COY. ... YELLOW.
"C" COY. ... BLUE.
"D" COY. ... RED.

Loads as follows:-

		Total per Company.
N.C.Os.	a Light load of Rockets and Flares	2 loads.
3 men	(8 Drums L.G. S.A.A. each	24 Drums.
	(3 Boxes Rifle Grenades	6 Boxes.
3 men	2 Boxes S.A.A. and 4 Drums L.G.	6 Boxes and 4 Drums.
5 men	10 tins water	50 tins.
Each man will carry 10 sandbags in addition		110 sandbags.

These Gangs will follow in rear of their Companies, and as soon as they have dumped their loads will be available for fighting. There is to be no movement in the rear other than that of Runners and Stretcher Bearers before ZERO plus 5 hours.

7. LEWIS GUNS.

2 Lewis Guns and 24 full drums of ammunition will remain at Battalion Headquarters. 2 Guns will be sent to Brigade Headquarters. No L.G. Personnel is required for these Guns.

8. ARTILLERY.

For Artillery barrage Time Table see Appendix "C".
The normal rate of advance of the creeping barrage will be 100 yards in 5 minutes, but the pace of the barrage will vary in order to conform with the advance of the ULSTER Division on the Left of the 25th DIVISION. Between the enemy's front and support lines it will be 100 yards in 1½ minutes.
2 New Zealand Batteries will bombard OZONE S.P. from ZERO to ZERO plus 14 minutes (this is in addition to our own bombardment).

9. MACHINE GUNS.

6 Guns of the 74th M.G.C. will be sited about 500 yards in rear of the British Front Line, and will form a portion of the Divisional M.G. Barrage assisting the Artillery. At ZERO 2 M.Gs. will advance with the rear wave of "A" Coy. Orders have been issued by the Brigade to the O.C. regarding the tactical handling of these guns.

10. TRENCH MORTARS.

2 STOKES will advance with the rear wave of "B" COY. Orders have been issued by the Brigade to the Officer Commanding as to the tactical handling of these Mortars.

11. BATTN. H.Q.

At ZERO hour, Company Headquarters in SURREY LANE, ZERO plus 30, UGLY RESERVE.
2 Headquarters Signallers and 2 Runners will go forward with the last wave of "A" COMPANY, and will establish themselves in UGLY RESERVE, and will then establish communication with Battalion Headquarters in SURREY LANE.

12. MEDICAL.

During assembly march to ZERO plus 15, Battalion Aid Post at Battalion Headquarters. ZERO plus 39 minutes - Junction of UGLY RESERVE and OZONE ALLEY where it will remain. A.D.M.S. is arranging to have 36 R.A.M.C. bearers at Brigade Advanced Dressing Station (POST ST. QUENTIN). These will move up to the old British Front Line at ZERO plus 30 minutes. From ZERO to ZERO plus 3 hours, Battn. Stretcher Bearers will be responsible for carrying wounded down to the old British Front Line. R.A.M.C. will arrange to evacuate from here. From ZERO plus 3 hours onwards, Battalion Stretcher Bearers will be responsible for carrying wounded back to OVAL. R.A.M.C. will arrange to evacuate from here.

13. **DRESS AND EQUIPMENT.** Fighting Order as per attached Table (Appendix "B").

14. **DUMPS.** Brigade Dump - T.6.c.3.6.

15. **PRISONERS & STRAGGLERS.** All Prisoners will be sent down under escort to Brigade Headquarters. The escort will not exceed 10 per cent of the personnel of each batch. Batches should not consist of less than 10. A receipt will be obtained for each Batch sent in. Full use will be made of carrying parties and slightly wounded.

The Regimental Police will establish Stragglers Posts of 1 N.C.O. and 2 men - (1). About Junction of TRALE AVENUE with DAY STREET. (2). Junction of SURREY LANE with MEDICINE HAT TRAIL.

At ZERO plus 1½ hours these Posts will move forward to Junction of SURREY LANE with British Front Line. These Posts will collect Stragglers into Squads and forward them to their Companies under a reliable Soldier. (Copies of orders for Stragglers for Battle Stragglers Posts, issued to N.C.Os. i/c. of Posts).

16. **COMMUNICATIONS:** The Signalling Officer will arrange for the system of communications and co-operation with contact aeroplanes as laid down in Appendix "B" of Brigade Operation Order.

17. **SYNCHRONISATION OF WATCHES.** Four Signallers will report to Brigade Signalling Officer at Brigade Battle Headquarters at ZERO minus 2 hours. (Brigade Battle Headquarters MIDLAND TRENCH), and will then communicate correct time to O.C. Companies.

18. **GENERAL.** All ranks are reminded they are fighting for:-
(i) The Allied cause of humanity against highly organised, disciplined, and educated savages.
(ii) For their women and children.
(iii) For the honour of IRELAND.

Victory depends on:-
(i) Suprise. To effect this there must be absolute silence during assembly and afterwards until ZERO.
(ii) Hugging the creeping barrage closely and cooly whilst strictly preserving formation.
(iii) Closest co-operation between all ranks of all arms.
(iv) Pace at which all Objectives after capture are secured, and favourable situations exploited to the full. Opportunities are often fleeting, quickness of decision and action is everything.
(v). Frequent, Brief, clear reports being received by Coy. and Battalion Commanders and Brigade Headquarters to enable opportunities and critical situations to be immediately dealt with.
(vi) The display of initiative and drive on the part of all ranks, and non-existence of the "Wait and SEE policy".
(vii) Hard, fast, determined scientific fighting.

WAR DIARY
2nd Bn. The Royal Irish Rifles
INTELLIGENCE SUMMARY

Volume II
SHEET 1
July 1917.

Place	Date	Hour	Summary of Events and Information	Remarks and references to Appendices
FRUGES	1st		Ref Map HAZEBROUCK Batln in billets — training carried out.	Ref Map Hazebrouck
	2		— do —	
	3		— do —	
	4		— do —	
	5		— do —	
	6		— do —	
	7		— do — Lieut. J.M. Boyle admitted to 39 Gen Hosp.	
RADINGHEM	8		Batln moved by route to RADINGHEM. Taking over billets from 9th J.N. Lancs.	
	9		Batln in billets. Brigade exercise carried out night 7/10th	
	10		— do —	
	11		— do — Capt Gallaher presented medals to the undermentioned through operation 7th–22nd at MESSINES. By gallantry etc. etc. M.C. 2/Lt J.Reilly M.Medal 7709 Rfn Curtins Lt A.Young- M.C. 2/Lt J.O'Shea M.M. 9098 Cpl Good W.S. M.M. 9362 L/Cpl D.C.M. 8003 Sgt O'Shea J. M.M. 8721 Sgt. Galloway T. M.M. 8257 Rfn Johnston Deputy M. M.M. 8721 Rfn Kavanagh J. M.M. 10791 Rfn McCabe W. M.M. M.M. 8915 Rfn Kavanagh J. M.M. 10791 Rfn McCabe W. M.M. 5257 Rfn Kernaghan H M.M. 10949 Rfn Caithness J. M.M. 8543 Rfn McIlrath W. M.M. 5770 Rfn Gamblet. M.M. 5111 Rfn Caldwell J. M.M.	

WAR DIARY or **INTELLIGENCE SUMMARY**

Army Form C. 2118.

France II 3rd Bn. The Royal Irish Rif.

SHEET 2. July 1917

Place	Date	Hour	Summary of Events and Information	Remarks and references to Appendices
RADINGHEM			The undermentioned .... were awarded honours and awards but were not present to receive them: Capt. T/Lt.Col. THOMPSON. D.S.O. No. 9397 Sergt. CONLAN. T. D.C.M. 8526 R/Cpl. FARRELL. A.M.M. 7165 Sgt. W. CROZIER M.M. No 6526 Cpl. BECKETT. W. .... D.C.M. .... in Belgium	R.A. Map Hazebrouck S/2 17/15E MAP 1917
RADINGHEM	12th		The Battalion marched to the vicinity of DELETTE & RECLINGHEM and carried out Brigade scenario in the afternoon. The Battalion bivouaced during the night 12/13th at Passaen Village. A draft of 102 other Ranks joined the Battalion	
RADINGHEM	13th		The exercise was repeated again and the Battalion returned to RADINGHEM in the Evening.	
RADINGHEM	14th		The Battalion moved by lorry & Transport to PIONEER CAMP. YPRES Area Map Reference Sheet 28 NW H 21 & 82. 1 O.R. W.I.A. Battalion arrived at Pioneer Camp night 14/15th working party 350	
Pioneer Camp	15th		proceeded to Huns and area Road Making	

Army Form C. 2118.

WAR DIARY or INTELLIGENCE SUMMARY

Volume II   2 Bn The Royal Irish Rifles

Sheet VII   July 1917

(Erase heading not required.)

Place	Date	Hour	Summary of Events and Information	Remarks and references to Appendices
PIONEER CAMP	16th		2nd Lieut G.D. Jones to Hospital. Night 16/17 Working party 460 working at same work. They had 15 Casualties. Capt Knox W.I.A. 2 O.R. K.I.A. 12 O.R. W.I.A.	
Pioneer Camp	17		Night 17/18 Working party of 200, Same work.	
PIONEER CAMP	18		Night 18/19 Working party of 250, same work, 2 O.R. W.I.A.	
PIONEER CAMP	19th		Night 19/20 Working party of 250. Same work	
PIONEER CAMP	20th		Night 20/21 Working party of 835 Same work	
PIONEER CAMP	21st		Night 21/22 Working party of 800. Same work. Attached Lieut P.C.V. Black R.A.M.C.	
PIONEER CAMP	22nd		Night 22/23 Working party 300 Same work	
do	23		" 23/24 " "	
do	24		" 24/25 " "	
do	25		Moved by route to Bivouacs at K 36 a 6.6 (Ry/Map Sheet 27) Capt R.D. JEFFARES rejoined Battn.	
K.36 a 6.6	26		Battn in Bivouacs	

Army Form C. 2118.

WAR DIARY
or
INTELLIGENCE SUMMARY

Volume II 2/3rd The Royal Scots Rifles
Sheet IV   July 1917

(Erase heading not required.)

Instructions regarding War Diaries and Intelligence Summaries are contained in F. S. Regs., Part II. and the Staff Manual respectively. Title Pages will be prepared in manuscript.

Place	Date	Hour	Summary of Events and Information	Remarks and references to Appendices
Sheet 27 Kabakis	27		Battn in Bivouac - training carried out. 70 O.R. reinforcements for Bn joined at I Corps Camp.	
	28		Battn in Bivouac. 2/Lieut C.R.W. McConnard joined - Lieut M.E. J. Moore and 21 OR joined 2nd Corps reinforcement camp.	Start? MW
	29		Battn moved by route to DOMINION CAMP G23 6.5.5.	
	30		Battn moved to SWAN CHATEAU 119c 7.5 - 280R draft from reinforcement camp joined Battn.	
	31		ZERO day - Battn was employed 2 Coys under 6 S & T3 and 2 Coys under 42nd A T Coy R.E. for work in connection of Communication track near HOOGE and Infantry bridge along MENIN ROAD from BIRR CROSS ROADS - Enemy shelling was heavy in the vicinity of HOOGE - 3OR W.I.A. 2/Lt YES MOORE MC joined & 50 OR from Corps reinforcement camp. Strength - fighting (exc Battn) 15 Off 450 OR	

R.S.M. Watkin Lieut & Adjt
R.S. Floyd
Lt Col Cmndg 2/3 The R.S.R.

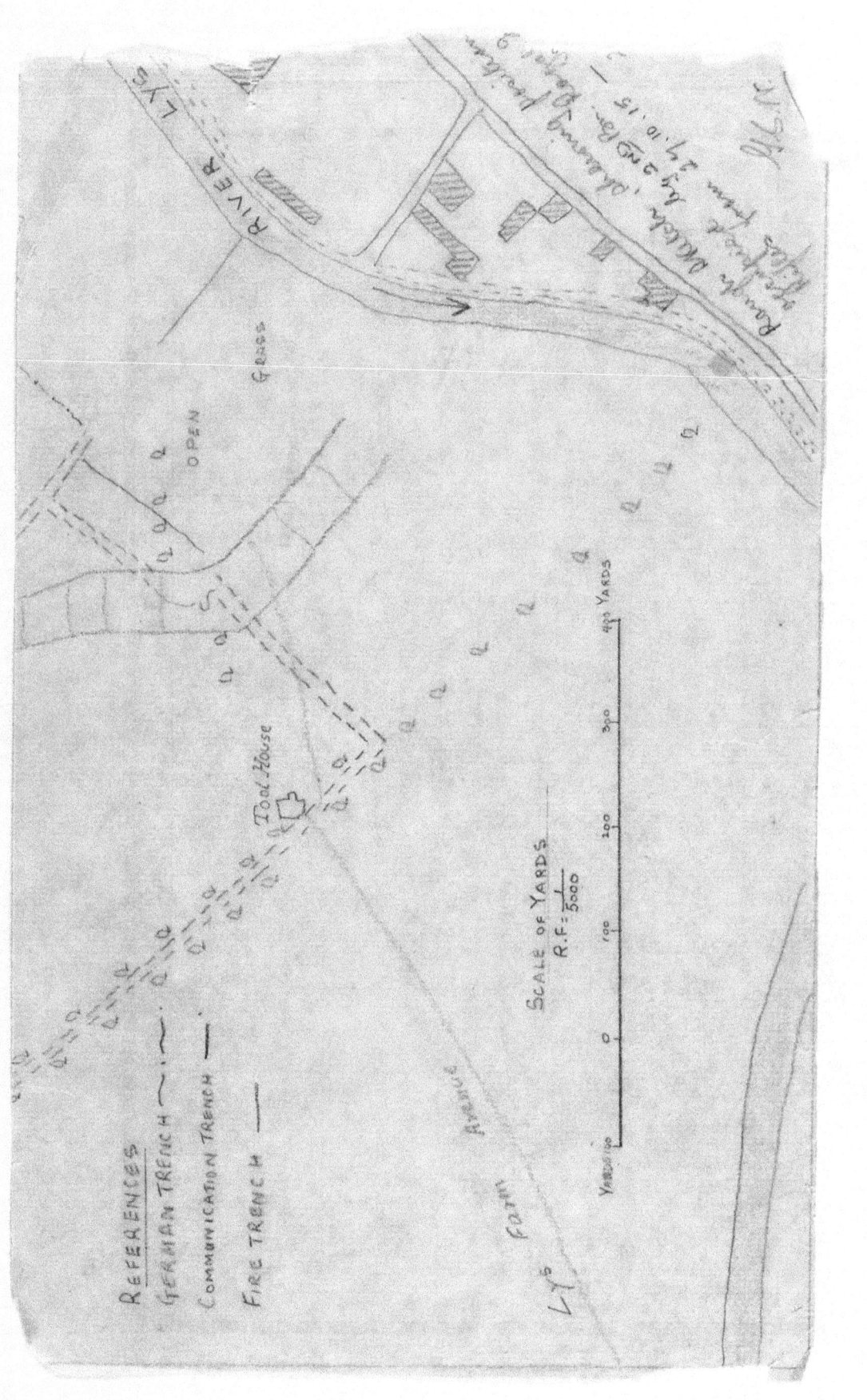

SECRET

OPERATION ORDER No 59
by
Major R. de R. Rose, Comdg. 2/Bn. R. I. Rifles

I. II Corps will capture at an early date, INVERNESS COPSE – GLENCORSE WOOD and the Southern end of the WESTHOEK RIDGE.

II. 74th Bde. will co-operate in the attack and will capture and consolidate approximate line – J.8.c.65.30. J.8.c.55.70 – J.8.a.40.55 – J.8.a.35.85 – J.2.c.10.00 – J.1.d.75.55.

III. The 2nd Bn. R.I.Rifles is detailed to capture and consolidate the BLACK LINE – J.8.a.55.75 – J.8.a.59.10 exclusive RED LINE J.8.a.35.75 exclusive – J.8.a.75.25 exclusive. The 13th CHESHIRES on RIGHT of Battalion and the 9th L.N.LANCS. on LEFT.

IV. The Batln. will attack in 4 waves. The 4th wave will consist of 'A' Coy. Remaining Coys. will attack in 3 waves in lines of Platoons in depth.

Objectives allotted to Coys. as under:–
'B' Coy. on the LEFT from J.8.a.35.75. to Roadway at J.8.a.40.55. exclusive.
'C' Coy. in centre from ROADWAY

T.8.a.40.55. inclusive to T.8.a.43.30. inclusive.
'D' Coy. from T.8.a.43.30. exclusive to T.8.a.50.10. exclusive.
'A' Coy. RED LINE from T.8.a.55.75. exclusive to T.8.a.75.29. exclusive.

5. For the attack Coys will form upon line - 'B' Coy. T.7.b.67.50 to T.7.b.65.30.
'C' Coy. from T.7.b.65.30. to T.7.b.70.05.
'D' Coy. from T.7.b.70.05 to T.7.d.70.95.
'A' Coy. from T.7.b.60.50 to T.7.d.75.96.

6. 'A' Coy. will proceed to RAILWAY WOOD when ordered and will be utilized to carry up rations and stores to purposes of line previous to the attack.

7. 2 Stokes Mortars will accompany 2nd Wave of the attack. One Gun is attached to 'B' Coy. and One to 'D' Coy.
O.C. Coys will select suitable positions for Guns in or near the BLACK LINE.

8. The Barrage will start at ZERO hour and will lift in accordance with attached map. Leading waves will conform to the line of the barrage and keep as close to it as possible.

IV

9. Detail Objective of waves -
1st and 2nd WAVES will push forward to capture and consolidate BLACK LINE less 2 Sections of 'B' Coy who will deal with Dugouts on either side of WESTHOEK CROSS ROADS and 2 sections of 'D' Coy who will assist 13th CHESHIRES to deal with Strong Point at J.8.c.15.95.
3rd WAVE will constitute a mopping party to mop up TABLER SUPPORT if necessary. ~~It will push on in keep to consolidate BLACK LINE~~ (See Supplement)
4th WAVE will capture and hold RED LINE.
10. Bn. H.Q. will be at J.7.d.65.90. All reports will be sent there.
11. MEDICAL AID POST will remain at present position.
12. DRESS - Battle Order as per APPENDIX 'A' with exception of 1st WAVE who will carry arms equipment and rations only. Packs of 1st WAVE will be dumped under Coy arrangements in vicinity of present position.
13. The Commdg. Officer is confident that the Batt. having done so well as

VIII

Copy No. 1

To:-
All Recipients of O.O. 59.

Reference para 9. and entry of WAVE add:-

Having completed the work will be collected by Officers present and work on construction of C.T. to BLACK LINE from T.7.B.94.07. to T.8.A.94.16. which will be taken by Engineers.

CONTACT PLANES

Contact Plane will pass over our line - (a) at daylight if attack takes place at night (B) if at dawn, at ZERO + 1 hour. Plane can be distinguished by 2 BLACK Plates underneath, when plane calls up on KLAXON HORN, or fires WHITE light White flares will be lit to show positions.

Every other man must carry a flare.

many forward more extensive operations, will on this occasion hug close to the barrage and ensure that all Objectives are gained without check.

14. ACKNOWLEDGE.

                                          Lieut

1/6/917   Adjutant 2/5n R. I. Rifles

Copies to: No 1 Comdg. Officer
           2 Coys + Coy HQ
           3 A Coy
           4 B
           5 C
           6 D
           7 44th Inf. Bde.

To:
All Recipients of O.O. 59.   Map Ref: HOOGE
                              EDITION 3 1:10000

Reference Operation Order No. 59. The following additions will be made:—

Waves will be formed up in jumping off position ~~1 hour 30 mts~~ before ZERO with the exception of three Posts per Coy. — One of which will be a Lewis Gun Post. These Posts will be withdrawn in time to take their places in the waves 30 minutes before ZERO.

Waves will move forward at 20 yards distance.

On gaining their Objectives, Coys will establish communication with units on their flanks.

Watches will be synchronized 2 h 5 ms before ZERO

TO BE DESTROYED AFTER CONTENTS ARE MASTERED.

C.F. Wilkin

1/8/1917.   Adjutant 11Bn. R.I. Rifles

SECRET

To:-
All Recipients of O.O.59.

Para. as under will be added to this Order:-

"ASSEMBLY"
"Men must be moved to Lines of assembly in driblets. Absolute silence must be maintained and no smoking allowed"

To para. 9 where it alludes to 4th WAVE, add
"Three Posts must be established in advance of RED LINE within limits of protective barrage to occupy points of vantage and cover consolidation. One must be a Lewis Gun Post, and house at J.8.B.90.70. appears to be a suitable position for it"

Army Form C. 2118.

WAR DIARY 2Bn The Royal Irish Rifles
or
INTELLIGENCE SUMMARY.
(Erase heading not required.)

Vol 32

Summary of Events and Information HOOGE August 1917.

Ref. Map Sheet 28 NW Sheet I

Place	Date	Hour	Summary of Events and Information	Remarks and references to Appendices
SWAN CHATEAU	1st		Battn in dugouts	
	2nd		— do —	
	3rd		— do —	
	4th		Battn moved into Ramparts at YPRES	
RAMPARTS YPRES	5		Battn in Ramparts YPRES	
			Battn moved into the line relieved 1Coy 10th WILTS Regt and 2 Coys 8th R.I.Rif. on WESTHOEK RIDGE. During move to trenches the enemy put down a heavy barrage about CHATEAU WOOD and BELLEWARDE RIDGE. A Coy were caught by the barrage while in CHATEAU WOOD. Rest two cross field at WISA O.R. 5.I.	
St Helena Mining Steben House	6		Battn in the line - Heavy intermittent shelling by Enemy - One German appeared about 1.10 am by B.Coy. 2nd Lieut S.J. Roy Roy Irish Rif. on Machine and R. Carpenters 3rd Roy I. Rif. and E.C. Stroham wounded very bad. 2nd Adolfus Kane K.I.P. 5 O.R. K.I.A. 2 O.R. D.o.W. 4th Roy I. Rif. James Parkin while Carpenters coming in and doing duty. 62 O.R. W.I.A. (inclusive two bad about)	

Army Form C. 2118.

Volume II 2nd Bn. The Royal Irish Rifles

Sheet 2

August 1917

WAR DIARY
or
INTELLIGENCE SUMMARY.

(Erase heading not required.)

Place	Date	Hour	Summary of Events and Information	Remarks and references to Appendices
In the Field	7th		Battn. holding the line. 2nd Lt. E. BROWN K.I.A.	
	8th		- do - Active operation orders to capture enemy's front line at 4.45am about 300x in advance of present line. ZERO hour to be at 4.45am.	
			9th. Room fell down. the enemy - operation was postponed for 24 hours. Battn. H.Q. moved forward to J7d 65.75 Bracelets.	
			2 O.R. K.I.A. 19 O.R. W.I.A.	
	9th		Battn. holding line – Orders received for active operation. Objectives and tasks as stated. O.O. 59 attached. ZERO hour was fixed for 4.35am 10th. Much preparatory work was needed and time so limited but assembly trenches were dug. much other work was finished in good time.	
	10th		Battn. were formed when to fasten to assembly by 3.5am. Small parties were left in the front line and withdrawn to hours before ZERO as ZERO hr. Battn. advanced to the attack. Two strong points (one to the supports at WESTHOEK) were quickly rushed by special parties detailed by Coys. and the enemy holding them taken or killed.	

WAR DIARY or INTELLIGENCE SUMMARY

Army Form C. 2118.

Volume I 2nd Battn Hetton & Rifles
Sheet 3   August 1917

warranted offered little resistance. He never pushed forward to JABBER SUPPORT. Most of the Enemy who were holding this line made no attempt to fight and fled at the sight of our men rushing through back on their front they were caught in our barrage and annihilated. An enemy M.G. which had just come into action on the left at J.7.60.60 was successfully dealt with by B.Coy 2nd L.t. McClendon leading a detachment rushed past the team of the gun to his right. The advance continued with the waves keeping close to the barrage and the troops chiefly grenades & rifles up enemy dugouts to which there were many, but in no case did the enemy show any real fight. The morale had been shaken by the effect of our weighty barrage and before he had time to collect himself our units were upon him. After the main objective had been reached (BLACK LINE) consolidation was proceeded with with vigour. A

WAR DIARY 2nd Battn The Royal Irish Rifles

Volume II Sheet 4

August 1917.

Army Form C. 2118.

Place	Date	Hour	Summary of Events and Information	Remarks and references to Appendices
			Line of posts was established from J8a 95.87 following 40m contour line & a few posts at J8a 92.25 immediately behind as protection through the enemy consolidation of Black line. Connection was established at once with 13th Cheshire Regt & 9th R. Innis on our right and left respectively. About 10 am Enemy was seen coming on ANZAC RIDGE and down forward slope towards HANNEBEEK valley first in sections and later in larger bodies presumably with the intention of massing for a counter attack. A message was sent back to this effect. This concentration continued throughout the day. About 3.30p.m. a feeble effort was made by the enemy but broke down under M.G. and rifle fire both the Lewis & artillery support which came later. About 7.30 p.m. more determined effort was made under cover of a short barrage and heavy bombardment of front line at WESTHOEK RIDGE. The S.O.S. signal was sent up	

A6915 Wt. W11422/M1160 350,000 12/16 D.D. & L. Forms/C./2118/14.

Army Form 'C. 2118.

Volume I   WAR DIARY
                                 or
Sheet 5   INTELLIGENCE SUMMARY.
                       (Erase heading not required.)

4th Bn The Royal Irish Rifles
August 1917

Place	Date	Hour	Summary of Events and Information	Remarks and references to Appendices

Our artillery did all reply. Shortly after, one of our aeroplanes appeared and dropped the S.O.S. Signal. Whereupon our artillery immediately put a heavy barrage. What aeroplane broke the attack+ is not actually known but this enemy were remnants which he sent forward. Many casualties were inflicted by M.G. fire before where remnants which he sent forward in all directions.

About 4.15 a.m. on the 11th the enemy broke forward strong Patrols only two of which reached our line. One Coy sent out about 12 O.R. got to within bombing distance and opened short on his Post it was quickly annihilated by bombs and afterwards this caused the other garrison of 10R. and 1 NCO. to keep firing at retiring to a dugout. A patrol was sent out and they surrendered without showing fight. The Battn was relieved on the line of capture on the night of 11-12th by 8th Border Regt Relief was completed at 4.15 a.m. Battn moved to YPRES and later appeared at HALIFAX CAMP at A.14.c.3.5.

Volume II WAR DIARY 2Bn 7th Royal Irish Rifles Army Form C. 2118.

Sheet 6 INTELLIGENCE SUMMARY. August 1917

Strength of Battn going into line 55 S.L.
16 Officers and 479 O.R.
Total casualties from 5th - 11th S.L.
8 Officers 30 O.R. K.I.A. 295 W.I.A. 17 Missing

Retail of Officer casualties.
Lieut A.B. Rt. Rene K.I.A. 5/8/17 Lieut E. Brown K.I.A. 9/10/1.7
Lieut B. Smitt'ee 2nd R.I.R.   "   13/8/17   "
Lieut Sir Morgan R.I. Rifles. "   "   "
Capt R.D. Jeffares 4th R.I.R. W.I.A.
Lieut R.S. Birkett 5th R.I.Rif.   "
 "   P.D. Alexander Rs. I.Rif.   "
 "   R. Carruthers 3rd R.I.R.   "
 "   B.J. Murphy 5th "   Missing

Strength of Battn coming out of the line
Officers 10 148 O.R.
Prisoners Captured 4 Officers (including 1 M.O.) and 150 O.R. 90 R.I.R.

WAR DIARY 1Bn. The Royal Irish Rifles

Army Form C. 2118.

VOLUME II Sheet 7.

INTELLIGENCE SUMMARY. August 1917

Ref Map SHEET 27 Sheet 28 NW

Place	Date	Hour	Summary of Events and Information	Remarks and references to Appendices
			Arms Captured :- One 77mm Gun & 5 M.G.S.	
	13th		Battn in huts Halifax Camp	
HALIFAX CAMP	14th		Battn moved by march route to STEENVOORDE.	
STEENVOORDE	15th		Battn in billets	
	16		— do —	
	17		Battn moved by march route to EECKE 21 OR draft joined	
EECKE	18		Training and in billets	
	19		— do —	
J.35.d.6.9	20		Battn moved by march route to STEENVOORDE AREA. Battn Hd.Qrs at J.35.d 6.9	
	21		Battn in billets - 74th Inf Bde inspected by C in Chief 50 OR draft joined	
STEENVOORDE	22		Battn in billets training carried out - Battn Hd.Qrs and 1 Coy moved to STEENVOORDE	
			16 OR draft joined.	
	23		In billets - training continued	
	24		— do —	
	25		— do —	

WAR DIARY 2/8th The Royal Irish Rifles

INTELLIGENCE SUMMARY

Volume II Sheet 7.

August 1917

Place	Date	Hour	Summary of Events and Information	Remarks and references to Appendices
STEENVOORDE	26		Refer to SHEET 27	SHEET 28 NN
	27		Drawing and billets	
	28		— do —	2 Lieut E.D. Jones Smash of Strength W.I.A. (Shell Shock) 16/7/17
	29		— do —	
	30		— do —	10 O.R. and joined
	31st		— do — Strength	25 Off. 5540.R.
			Trench	10 " 289 " (Including 82...)

W.R. Smith Lieut Col
Commanding 2/8 R. Ir. Rifles

WAR DIARY or INTELLIGENCE SUMMARY

Army Form C. 2118.

2nd Bn. McRoy. 8 Rifles

Volume II 74/25

Sheet 1.

September 1917

Sheet 27. V 33

(Erase heading not required.)

Place	Date	Hour	Summary of Events and Information	Remarks and references to Appendices
STEENVOORDE	1st		Ref. Map Hazebrouck 5-A	
	2nd		Batt. moved by m.t. to北 march to CORNWALL CAMP near OUDERDOM.	
			Batt. in Camp. At 5.30 p.m. Batt. ordered by Bde. to move to line – 11.30 p.m. Bn.	
			moved on route to the line taking over Sector from J 8 a 47.55	
			to J 2 C 16.55 with 2/3rd London Regt. on WESTHOEK RIDGE. 2/B.C.	
			Coy in front line (Mr Danielch) and D Coy in Support (2nd Lt)	
			Relief was completed at 11.30 p.m.	
			Strength going into the line 10 Off 242 OR	
3			Batt. holding line. Patrols sent out during night.	
4			do	enemy aircraft
5			do	active over our lines – Enemy artillery more active on Sector
	6		Dell holding line @ 7.30 a.m. Enemy in front opened 3 very heavy barrage on	
			Batt's left & the line above sector held by troops on the	
			flanking Bde. our left. The above was quickly taken &	
			attack. Artillery support was called for by S.O.S. and	
			broke rifle and m-gun fire was opened on the		34

WAR DIARY or INTELLIGENCE SUMMARY

Army Form C. 2118.

Volume VI 2nd Bn. The Royal Irish Rifles September 1917

Sheet 2 Sheet 28

Place	Date	Hour	Summary of Events and Information	Remarks and references to Appendices
Anzefrank	5		advancing enemy infantry to front line. Enjd. she portrayed had suffered little from our artillery barrage. The attack quickly matted away. Have & the enemy reached our lines	
			Artillery activity continued till about 5.45pm then went very quiet. Six patrols were sent out during the night but no information was gained. 1 Patrol	
	7		reported attacked, very quiet in line. Aircraft (enemy) active. He would hardly send over at all.	
	8		Batt. in line & relieved by 20th B. Fusilier Regt.	
	9		Relief completed about 2.30am. Bn moved by route march to MICMAC CAMP 4/3/6 3/6 total casualties during from the 2nd OR 3 KIA 19 WIA 1 missing. Capt J.C.C.Thompson "A" Coy injured.	
MICMAC	10		Batt. in camp	
CAESTRE	11		Batt moved by bus to CAESTRE area 9 OR wht joined	
STEENBECQUE	12		Batt moved by route to STEENBECQUE	

WAR DIARY or INTELLIGENCE SUMMARY
Army Form C. 2118

Volume II 7th Battalion Kings Liverpool Rifles
September 1917
Sheet #3   Sheet 36 b

Place	Date	Hour	Summary of Events and Information	Remarks and references to Appendices
RAMBERT	13th		Hazebrouck 5th Battn. moved by route to RAMBERT (ROCHEL AREA)	
	14th		Rest in billets - Training Commenced 37 OR attached joined	
	15th		- do - - do - Entrained	
	16th		- do - - do -	
	17th		- do - - do -	
	18th		- do - - do - Capt. E Stanley Jones	
	19th		- do - - do -	
	20th		- do - - do -	
	21st		- do - - do -	
	22nd		- do - - do -	
	23rd		- do - - do - 24 OR Regt joined	
	24th		- do - - do - 4 OR " "	
	25th		- do - - do - Strength 8 — OR	
	26th		25 Division the - do - - do - 26 669	
	27th		Batn. in Billets - do - - do - 13 404	
	28th		- do - - do - Br. ot " entrained on 26.9.17	
	29th		- do - - do -	
	30th			

PATROL REPORTS.

Division.	Strength of Patrol.	Time and Date.	Objective or Task.	Remarks and information.
25th Division. 74th Brigade. 9th L.N.Lancs.	2nd Lieut F.H. BUNTING & 8 other ranks.	9.5 p.m. † 12.30 a.m. 7th/8th.	1. To obtain a prisoner. 2. To obtain identification from dead reported by previous night's patrol. 3. Locate enemy positions.	Patrol went out at 9 p.m. None of the enemy were seen whilst out, but sketch attached gives approximate positions we were fired at from. One of the enemy dead was in a large shell hole which was half full of water, and no identification could be obtained. There was a hasty wire entanglement in front of JABBER RESERVE which was badly knocked about. Patrol reports hearing the shouts of enemy wounded after a few rounds of shrapnel from our 18 Pdrs.
25th Division. 74th Brigade. 9th L.N.Lancs.	2nd Lt.W.D.JAMES & 9 other ranks.	10.5 p.m. – 1.15 a.m. 7th/8th.	1. Capture a prisoner. 2. To obtain identification from enemy dead lying in front of our line. 3. Obtain location of enemy posts.	Patrol left right flank flank posts of Battalion (J.8.a.75.10) and proceeding in a N.E. direction suddenly came under fire from an enemy machine gun which was approximately 500 yards away at J.8.d.1.9. Patrol then struck north for about 50 yards and came close to some dugouts which were occupied by the enemy. The ground here was very marshy. About 100 yards further north of the dugouts was a post occupied by the enemy from which he was firing flares. Only 1 dead German was seen and no identification was possible, he having been dead about a month.
25th Division. 74th Brigade. 2nd R.I.Rifles.	Cpl O'KANE & 6 other ranks.	11.30 p.m. – 1.30 a.m. 7th/8th.	To capture a prisoner dead or alive.	Patrol left front line at J.2.b.30.25 and proceeded via old house at J.2.c.45.30 to corner of hedge at J.2.c.50.35. At this point patrol leader posted some men along west side of hedge and with 1 man crept through gap and laid down about 10 yards on east side of hedge. Patrol was working in conjunction with another patrol on its immediate right under A/C.S.M. GIBSON. In the event of a shot being fired from that patrol, instructions were to open fire also on any of the enemy seen moving, and to watch house held by enemy at J.2.c.57.39. Sounds of work could be heard coming from the far side of the house from where patrol was posted. During the time it was out the enemy kept putting up numerous very lights in all directions towards our lines. Patrol withdrew at 1.45 a.m.

Division.	Strength of Patrol.	Time and Date.	Objective or task.	Remarks and information.
25th Division. 74th Brigade. 2nd R.I.Rifles.	A/C.S.M.GIBSON & 6 O.Rs.	11.50 p.m. - 1.30 a.m. 7th/8th.	Capture a prisoner dead or alive.	Patrol left the front line at J.2.c.45.10 Following marked line of hedge which runs N.E. from J.2.c.45.15 to road. About 10 yards from commencement of hedge, patrol struck an old C.T. which they followed to where it ended at J.2.c.55.25. Reaching end of C.T. a lookout was posted on right side of hedge about J.2.c.60.27 - posting the remaining men in corner where the hedge is met by another one running N.W. Patrol then proceeded on towards the road as far as J.2.c.65.30 where it remained for about ½ hour. During the time it was there it saw a lot of movement of the enemy from J.2.c.90.35 along a trench running N.W. parallel to the road - between 20 & 30 men were working in it. It remained listening and watching until 1.30 a.m. when it withdrew. During the time it was out about 12 Very lights were thrown up from the enemy's positions. No freshly put out wire in front of enemy was seen.
25th Division. 74th Brigade. 2nd R.I.Rifles.	Cpl WINSTANLEY & 6 O.Ranks.	9 p.m. - 2 a.m. 7th/8th.	Capture a prisoner dead or alive.	Patrol left the front line about J.8.a.50.95 and proceeded N.E. through two hedges towards road for about 100 yds where it turned sharp to the right and lay down about J.2.c.70.30. On its way to this point just after having passed through the first hedge, shouts and noises were heard from the enemy's direction, which seemed to come from straight in front. Patrol waited until 2 a.m., at which time it withdrew, not having seen anything of the enemy. During the time it was out, enemy threw up about 3 Very Lights which seemed to come from behind hedge at J.2.c.80.30 running S.E. parallel with road.

Division.	Strength of Patrol.	Time and Date.	Objective or task.	Remarks or Information.
25th Division. 74th Brigade. 2nd R.I.Rifles.	Sergeant KEENE 6 O.Rs.	9 p.m. 7/9/17.	To capture a prisoner.	Patrol proceeded from J.2.c.35.95 at 9 p.m. and moved forward to about 15 yards south of old house at J.2.c.65.35 where it lay in wait for about 1½ hours and then withdrew as it had been ordered to return by 11 p.m. No sign of the enemy was seen. Very lights were fired from trench which is heavily wired about 300 yards to the front. No dead bodies could be found.

NOMINAL ROLL OF OFFICERS AND OTHER RANKS GRANTED AWARDS DURING WESTHOEK OPERATION

	MAJOR R de R. ROSE.	M.C.
	CAPTAIN J.B. McAREVEY.	M.C.
	CAPTAIN T. McALINDON.	M.C.
	CAPTAIN G.F. LINDSAY. R.A.M.C.	M.C.
	2ND LIEUT. T.C. WALLIS.	M.C.
	2ND LIEUT. R.S. WALSH.	M.C.
9649	Q.M.S. TURNER J.J.	M.M.
9927	SGT. WALSH J.	M.M.
4951	SGT. BELLIS G.	D.C.M.
6720	SGT. WHELAN J.	M.M.
4953	SGT. BEVAN R.	M.M.
7674	L/SGT. McFARLAND A.	M.M.
8582	SGT. SMITH J.	M.M.
5121	CPL. ROBERTS T.	M.M.
9996	L/C SHERIDAN F.	M.M.
4981	L/C CLARKE L.	M.M.
8593	L/C SINCLAIR G.	M.M.
7104	L/C SMYTH J.	M.M.
8722	L/C McTEAGUE T.	D.C.M.
6436	L/C WRIGHT J.	D.C.M.
6782	RFN. KILEEN P.	M.M.
4536	RFN. HALL T.	M.M.
5717	RFN. COSTELLO R.	M.M.
42617	RFN. HOFFMAN S.	M.M.
6928	RFN. SMYTH J.	M.M.
5937	RFN. FAY T.	M.M.
10411	RFN. McDERMOTT J.	M.M.
43592	RFN. OATWAY W.	M.M.
1525	RFN. SALT W.H.	M.M.
7795	RFN. ATKINSON A.	M.M.
43023	RFN. COURTNEY T.	M.M.
4948	RFN. BARTABY E.	M.M.
5219	RFN. ROBERTS J.	M.M.
9583	RFN. QUIGLEY H.	M.M.
6781	RFN. O'GARA M.	M.M.
44135	RFN. QUARTERMAN H.	M.M.

(To 36 5?)

Volume I

WAR DIARY
or
INTELLIGENCE SUMMARY

Army Form C. 2118.

2nd Bn the Royal Irish Rifles
October 1917

Sheet Vol 34

Place	Date	Hour	Summary of Events and Information	Remarks and references to Appendices
RAIMBERT	1st		Lt Major Angebrant G.O. 2/W	35
	2		Battn in billets - training carried out.	
	3		- do -	
	4th		- do -	
BETHUNE	5th		Battn moved by Route to BETHUNE	
			Battn moved into the line relieving 22nd Bn The Royal ?? Fusrs) C to D Coy	
	6th		in the CAMBRIN SECTOR (from))	
			Front Line H+B Coy's in Support.	
			Battn relief done Capt R.T. Jefferies Dep'ut 2nd Lt H.Proctor	
			and Lt R. Anstey joined.	
	7		Battn in line.	
	8		- do -	
	9		- do -	
	10		- do - 1 OR. WIA 2 OR. WIA (wnds) 2 OR. W. (S/W)	
	11		- do -	
	12		Bn relieved by 13th Cheshire Regt and moved to billets into support 3rd Army	
			Bn H.Q. to ANNEQUIN One Coy to Class Support in Factory dugouts	

Volume 5

WAR DIARY 9/Bn. The Royal Scots and 9/Bn Army Form C. 2118.
or
INTELLIGENCE SUMMARY. Sheet 2 October 1917

Place	Date	Hour	Summary of Events and Information	Remarks and references to Appendices
ANNEQUIN	13th		Battn in Support	
	14th		— do —	
	15th		— do — 1 O.R. relieved Co'y at FACTORY DUGOUTS.	
	16th		— do — 1 O.R. W.I.A.	
	17th		— do —	
	18th		Battn moved into the line relieving 13th Bn. the Cheshire Regiment. Scout sector on ceased front 6th-12th inst. Relief complete at 4.45pm. 1 Company Portuguese R.I. attached and posted into line as Bn in Evacuation. C & D Coy front line. A & B Coy Support. Patrols sent out.	
In the Line	19th		Battn in the line. Patrols sent out at night.	
	20th		—do—	
	21st		Capt C.F. Williams MC. proceeded to H.Q. XI Corps to be attached thereto. Battn in line. Lieut A.H. Liffen, 3rd Bn R.S. Rif., 2/Lt C. Rule, 3rd Bn R.S. Rif. and 2/Lt F.G. Stewart, 3rd Bn R.S. Rif and draft of 62 O.R. joined. Patrols sent out into Coy Salient A Salvory C, and B relieving D.	

WAR DIARY
or
INTELLIGENCE SUMMARY.
(Erase heading not required.)

Army Form C. 2118.

2nd Bn. The Royal Irish Rifles.
October 1917.

Volume II   Sheet 3

Place	Date	Hour	Summary of Events and Information	Remarks and references to Appendices
In the Line.	22nd		Battn in line. Patrols sent out under 2/Lt A Dawson and 2nd Lt C.R.W. A Command.	
	23rd		Battn in line. Patrol under 2/Lt A Dawson consisting of this Officer and 8 other ranks reported missing. No sign of them could be seen during the day. About 7.15pm three men of the patrol succeeded in regaining our lines. Patrols under 2/Lt J.R. Rowland and 2/Lt L.C. Wallis D.C. went out to try and find traces but were unsuccessful. (Casualties 2/Lt A Dawson and 5 O.R. missing). Enemy Artillery and T.M's unusually active on front line. OLD BOOTS Trench and C.T.o. Battn relieved in line by 13th Bn the Cheshire Regt. Relief complete 4 p.m. A and B Coys and Bn H.Q moved by route to BEUVRY, (Bn HQ BETHUNE Ambrecourt By F.14.a.2.2). C and D Coys to ANNEQUIN. Patrol under 2/Lt J.S. Stanley went out from 13th Cheshire line, after preparatory fire by STOKES T.M. & tr/y and red Crossed of Money. Patrol saw Rifles identified no belonging to Ewe of the O.R. missing were found.	
	24th			

Army Form C. 2118.

2nd Bn. the Royal Irish Rifles

October 1917

WAR DIARY
or
INTELLIGENCE SUMMARY.
(Erase heading not required.)

Volume II.   Sheet 4

Place	Date	Hour	Summary of Events and Information	Remarks and references to Appendices
BEUVRY	25th		Battalion in reserve. A + B Coys and H.Q. at BEUVRY. "C" and D Coys at ANNEQUIN. Patrol consisting of 1 N.C.O., 4 O.R.s and 6 other ranks went out from 1st Cheshires front to try and find further traces of enemy Patrol about the place where 2nd Lt. J.P. Potely had found the rifles the previous night. No further trace was found.	
	26th		Battn in reserve. Working Party to bury cable between CAMBRIN and ANNEQUIN. 'C' and 'D' Coys relieved from ANNEQUIN to BEUVRY by north and were billeted in BEUVRY by about 5 p.m. 2/Lt Percy Phillips 5th Bn. Royal Irish Rifles joined the Battn. Battn in reserve. Working Parties continued.	
	27th		do.	
	28th		do.	
	29th		do.	
	30th		do.	
	31st		Battn moved into the line relieving 13th Bn. the Cheshire Regiment, in CAMBRIN LEFT Sector. Relief complete at 4.20 p.m. C and D Coys front line (Right and left respectively), A and B Coys Support line. Trench strength. Officers 21 Other ranks 491.	

W. Goodman Lt. Col.
Comdg 2nd Bn. the Royal Irish Rifles

LIST OF OFFICERS OF "POINTER"

GOING INTO ACTION

HEADQUARTERS.

1. Lieut-Col. H.R. Goodman. — Commanding.
2. Lieut. R.A. Young. — Signalling Officer.
3. 2nd Lieut. G.D.J. Jones. — Asst Adjutant.
4. Lieut. A.B. Ross. — Medical Officer.

"A" COMPANY.

1. Captain W.W. MacKeown. — Commanding Coy.
2. 2nd Lieut. P. McMahon. — 2nd in Command.
3. 2nd Lieut. S.J.V. O'Brien.
4. 2nd Lieut. S. Mercer.

"B" COMPANY.

1. Captain T.J.C.C. Thompson. — Commanding Coy.
2. Lieut. E. Brown. — 2nd in Command.
3. 2nd Lieut. W. Dobbie.
4. 2nd Lieut. R.S.H. Noble.
5. 2nd Lieut. W.H. Calwell.

"C" COMPANY.

1. 2nd Lieut. A.M. Anderson. — Commanding Coy.
2. 2nd Lieut. H. Marshall.
3. 2nd Lieut. W. Rainey. — 2nd in Command.
4. 2nd Lieut. E.J. Williams.

"D" COMPANY.

1. 2nd Lieut. G.F. Fry. — Commanding Company.
2. 2nd Lieut. L.J. Ricks. — 2nd in Command.
3. 2nd Lieut. H.C. Mallett.
4. 2nd Lieut. T.C. Wallis.

APPENDIX "A".

STORES IN BRIGADE DUMP.

T.6.c.3.6.

S.A.A.	100 Boxes.
MILLS No.5	400 "
MILLS No.23	200 "
Sandbags	10,000.
Wire, barbed	100 Coils.
Stakes, corkscrew, Short and Long	500.
STOKES ammunition	500 rounds.
VERY LIGHT AMMN.	20 Boxes 1". 10 " 1½".
KNIFE RESTS, collapsible	300.

APPENDIX "B".

FIGHTING ORDER.

1. Packs will contain the following:-
   (1). Unexpired portion of the days rations.
   (2). Iron Rations.
   (3). Soap and Towel.
   (4). Pair of Laces.
   (5). Shaving Kit.
   (6). Pair of Socks.
   (7). Canteen.

2. Waterproof sheets will be carried inside packs.

3. Supporting Straps of packs to be worn.

4. Each man will carry:-
   (1). 170 Rounds S.A.A.
   (2). 2 Sandbags.
   (3). 2 Bombs. (Men of Bombing Squad 8 bombs each, except carriers, 12 each. Rifle Grenade men each to carry 8 Rifle Grenades and 12 rounds of Special Blank Cartridge. S.A.A. to be reduced in these cases to 60 rounds).
   (4). Steel Helmets will be painted.
   (5). Box Respirator.
   (6). Field Dressing.
   (7). All Water Bottles must be filled.
   (8). Men must be cautioned to use their rations and water sparingly, as it is probable they will go 48 hours at least on the rations carried in their packs.
   (9). In addition to the above, Companies must be in possession of:-
       (a). Wire Cutters - 12 per Platoon, which must be attached to the person or rifle.
       (b). 12 pairs Hedging Gloves per Company, which must be tied to the left wrist.
       (c). 2 Black and Yellow Distinguishing Flags per Platoon.
       (d). Grenadiers, Mills Grenade Extracting Hook.
           Arrangements must be made for carrying these.

   (10). Officers will carry all available Very Light Pistols, and 5 rounds S.O.S. Very Light Ammunition (RED) and 10 white. Officers Servants will carry 5 rounds RED and 15 white. Each N.C.O. will carry a Flare.

   (11). Tools - Regimental. Each Lewis Gun Team 1 Shovel. Bombers and Rifle Grenadiers - Nil. Riflemen 1 pick to 4 shovels strapped on packs.

   (12). 24 Bill Hooks per Battalion.

NOTE.
   (a). Blank ammunition for Rifle Grenades must be kept separate from ball ammunition.
   (b). Each Grenadier should carry a piece of oily rag for oiling rods just before use.
   (c). Each Platoon to carry 2 'P' Bombs, to be used under supervision of O.C. Platoon, only if other means to clear dugouts fail.

   All men of Rifle Section to carry a Pick or a Shovel. 1 Pick to 4 Shovels.

APPENDIX "C".

ORDERS FOR BATTLE STRAGGLERS POSTS.

1. Collect all stragglers (armed and unarmed) seen moving to the rear through the line of posts. Stragglers will be re-armed with rifles and ammunition taken from the wounded, or from the nearest Advanced Dressing Station. Stragglers will be re-formed under cover, or at the Divisional Collecting Station and sent forward as circumstances permit.

2. Every man on battle straggler post duty should know the position of the Posts on his right and left, the nearest dressing station, field ambulance, and the collecting stations for stragglers and for Prisoners of War, and the nearest way to them. He should know where the A.P.M. is to be found.

3. All wounded men, and those who appear to be suffering from gas poisoning, will be taken to the nearest advanced dressing station, or to the Divisional Collecting Station, unless they can produce a printed Medical tally, shewing the nature of the wound, or disability, in which case they are to be allowed to proceed.

4. Examine all individual N.C.Os. and men passing to and from the trenches both by day and by night, and ascertain their business. Sacks and bundles carried by men coming from the trenches are to be examined, and if found to contain plunder the men are to be arrested, and either handcuffed or placed in close confinement. Men in possession of Revolvers or Field Glasses which look like the property of officers are to be detained pending investigation.

5. Ascertain the names and units of all Officers passing the post at night.

6. Prevent all civilians from passing the line of posts towards the front. Arrest all civilians seen coming from the direction of the front, and hand them over to the French Gendarmes. If their behaviour excites suspicion they are to be searched. All papers, etc., found on them are to be tied into a packet and handed over to the Gendarmes or Military Police. No passes are to be accepted from civilians under any circumstances.

7. Arrest all civilians found wandering about in the vicinity of the line of posts between 8 p.m. and 5 a.m.

8. Officers and men in French uniform are not to be allowed to pass the line unless in possession of a pass.

9. Control the traffic at the post, seeing that cross roads are kept clear for reinforcing troops, and that loaded ammunition carts or lorries, supply vehicles or ambulances are given a clear passage.
    The intervals between the posts are to be patrolled at uncertain times both by day and by night.
    The first Stragglers to come in should be retained to assist battle posts, if it appears that large numbers of stragglers will have to be dealt with.

Copy issued to N.C.Os. i/c. Posts.

APPENDIX "C".

ARTILLERY BARRAGE TIME TABLE.

1. At ZERO an intense Barrage will be put down on enemy front line (NUTMEG and UGLY TRENCHES)

2. The Barrage will lift of the various enemy lines and S.Ps. and infantry will capture same at the following times:-

    All objectives on the same line must be taken simultaneously:-

(a). NUTMEG and UGLY TRENCHES.   (Yellow Line).   ZERO plus 3½ minutes.
(b). NUTMEG and UGLY SUPPORT.   ZERO plus 5 minutes.
(c). NUTMEG and UGLY RESERVES   (Grey Line)   ZERO plus 7 minutes.
(d). NUTMEG and UGLY LANE   ZERO plus 12 minutes.
(e). OZONE STRONG POINT   ZERO plus 16 minutes.
(f). Along STEENBEKE where it crosses OZONE
     ALLEY to the ROAD O.31.a.80.13. (Pink Line)   ZERO plus 30 minutes.
(g). SLOPING ROOF TRENCH   (Purple Line)   ZERO plus 57 minutes.
(h). INTERMEDIATE TRENCH   ZERO plus 1 hour 17 minutes.
(i). OCTOBER TRENCH   (Orange Line)   ZERO plus 1 hour 40 minutes.
(j). OCTOBER SUPPORT   (Blue dotted Line) ZERO plus 1 hour 55 minutes.
(k). OCTOBER ALLEY   (Blue Line)   ZERO plus 2 hours 16 minutes.
(l). OCTOBER AVENUE   (Black Line)   ZERO plus 4 hours 10 minutes.
(m). LINE OF STRONG POINTS (Black dotted Line)   ZERO plus 5 hours 30 minutes.
(n). ODIOUS, ODD & OWL TRENCHES (Green Line).   ZERO plus 10 hours 20 minutes.

APPENDIX "I".

COY.	OBJECTIVE.	SPECIAL POINTS TO BE DEALT WITH.	CONSOLIDATION TASKS.
"A"	O.P. and DUGOUTS about OZOR S.E. (6.31.d.28.30) and ZINA HILL.	Strong Point at O.31.d.25.30.	1 Platoon clearing Battalion's Sector of DUGOUTS of all arms and making it passable for Infantry. 2 Platoons constructing S.P. at O.31.d.25.30
"B"	ONLAND LANE, OZOR ALLEY, JUNCTION of OZOR ALLEY and OZONE TRENCH.	OZOR ALLEY.	Mopping up of dugouts at OZONE TRENCH and up ground to 100 yards North of OZOR ALLEY. On completion of Mopping up, wiring and digging a C.T. from O.31.d.50.50 (junction of OZOR ALLEY and OZONE TRENCH) to O.31.d.85.50 (just North of PLAYING FIELD ROAD FARM).
"C"	UGLY TRENCH, UGLY CORNER, COY. SUPPORT, UGLY LANE.		SAPPERS. 1 Platoon to mop up UGLY TRENCH and UGLY CORNER. 1 Platoon to mop up UGLY SUPPORT. 1 Platoon in reserve.
"D"	UGLY TRENCH, UGLY SUPPORT, UGLY LANE, KARNAK, BOMBAY.	O.P. and DUGOUTS in OVAL.	1 Platoon to mop up its Sector of UGLY LANE. 1 Platoon to mop up its Sector of KARNAK. 1 Platoon to mop up Dugouts in OVAL.

W095/2247/2

25TH DIVISION
74TH INFY BDE

3RD BN WORCESTER REGT
Nov 1917 – MAY 1918

From 7 Bde Same Div

To 19 DIV. 57 Bde

WAR DIARY
or
INTELLIGENCE SUMMARY.

Army Form C. 2118.

25th Divn — 7th Foresters Regt.

VM 39

September 1917

Place	Date 1917	Hour	Summary of Events and Information	Remarks and references to Appendices
TRENCHES GIVENCHY FESTUBERT SECTOR M.1 36 S.W.3 S.2.c.35.15 to 36 N.W.1 A.5.d.95.55	1 to 3		The Battalion completed an uneventful tour in the trenches. Retaliation shots by our artillery were carried out for one round during the mornings of the 1st, 2nd & 3rd opposite the front of the Battalion inmediately on our right. In retaliation the enemy shelled and trench mortared our front line in the vicinity of BARNTON TRENCH.	A.N.C
WINDY CORNER M.1 36 N.W.1 A.BC&C40	4	3 p.m.	The Bn was relieved by the 8th Loyal North Lancashire Regt. and moved back into Bde. support at WINDY CORNER. B Co. garrisoned the GIVENCHY defences, and A Co. moved to the OLD BRITISH FRONT LINE. The Co. of the 2 South Staffordshire Regt. returned to their own unit immediately after relief.	A.N.C.
"	5 6 9		In support at WINDY CORNER. Working parties amounting to two Coys per day formed daily during this period.	F.B.C.
ANNEQUIN	10		On this date the Bn was transferred from the 7th Inf. Bde. to the 74th Inf. Bde. The Bn had been in the 7th Inf. Bde. over six years, and had fought on that formation during the war and to dy. the reason for of the transfer was to replace the 2nd Royal Irish Rifles, which moved to the 36th Division. The Bn. relieved them at ANNEQUIN in the afternoon.	

Army Form C. 2118.

WAR DIARY
or
INTELLIGENCE SUMMARY.
(Erase heading not required.)

Instructions regarding War Diaries and Intelligence Summaries are contained in F.S. Regs., Part II. and the Staff Manual respectively. Title pages will be prepared in manuscript.

November 1917

Place	Date 1917	Hour	Summary of Events and Information	Remarks and references to Appendices
ANNEQUIN	11		Whilst at ANNEQUIN the Battalion was in Brit. Support. The 7th & 9th Bn. was holding the CAMBRIN SECTOR, with the 11th Lancashire Fusiliers and 13th Cheshires in the line, on the right and left respectively. The 9th Loyal North Lancashire Regt. was in reserve at BEUVRY. D Co. of the Battalion was in FACTORY DUGOUTS.	H.N.C.
— ʺ —	12 to 15		The Battalion found working parties daily for the forward area, except on the 18th [?] on this date G.O.C. Brigade inspected the Battalion, and welcomed their arrival in the 7th & 9th Bn.	R.S.L.
TRENCHES CAMBRIN RIGHT SUB-SECTOR	16 to 23		The Bn. relieved the 11th Lancashire Fusiliers in the front line. On one night were the 1/5th Sherwood Forester's, and on one left the Kensingtons. There was an unsuccessful raid made to secure an identification by means of energetic patrolling, but met with no success. An officer's patrol located the German trenches at one point, but found none of the enemy. Other enemy activity was chiefly confined to 'knee-rifles' in the front line. On the afternoon of the 22nd 23rd enemy shells were received by Battn. Hd. Quarters.	
ANNEQUIN	23		Relieved by the 9th Royal North Lancashire Regt. & Bn. & Bn. ce ANNEQUIN	J.M.L.

WAR DIARY
or
INTELLIGENCE SUMMARY.

(Erase heading not required.)

Army Form C. 2118.

November 1917

Place	Date 1917	Hour	Summary of Events and Information	Remarks and references to Appendices
ANNEQUIN	24 & 25		Nothing to report. Very pleasant weather.	
BEUVRY	26		The Bn moved back to rest at BEUVRY, relieving the 2 R Monmouth Fusiliers.	
"	27 & 28		No working parties found from Bens. Recovery carried out during the mornings. Football played in afternoons.	
TRENCHES CAMBRIN RIGHT SUB SECTOR	29			
	30	2.30 p.m.	In the evening the Bn relieved the 9th Royal South Lancashire Regt. The outgoing battalion reported that the evening artillery had been increasingly active. At this hour the enemy opened a very heavy bombardment with "incendiary" in the front line, and with H.E. on the support area. The bombardment lasted about half an hour after which a party of Germans entered the [illegible] left company front (A Co.) but were immediately ejected. The enemy threw a few stick bombs, but during retired on being encountered by Capt Unitt 2/Lt BRETTELL and a small party of [illegible]. One of the enemy was killed, and his body remained in our somewhat serious [illegible]. 2/Lt BRETTELL, during the long night watch [illegible].	
		7.5 p.m.	Enemy bombarded or threatened on the Canal front, i.e. the whole Battalion front. Here the bombardment was heavier	

A5834 Wt. W4973/M687 750,000 8/16 D. D. & L. Ltd. Forms/C.2118/13

WAR DIARY
or
INTELLIGENCE SUMMARY.
(Erase heading not required.)

Army Form C. 2118.

Place	Date	Hour	Summary of Events and Information	Remarks and references to Appendices
TRENCHES RIGHT SUB-SECTOR CAMBRIN	Oct 1917		and lasted until 7.50 p.m. The enemy again left his trenches opposite the left company but was stopped by a Lewis gun standing patrol pushed out in front of our lines. The barrage down was very considerable and the trenches in several places had disappeared.	Pearton Lt Col. Cmdg 3/ Worcestershire Regt

Casualties during November 1917

Dates	Officers			Total Officers	Other Ranks			Total Other Ranks	Remarks
	K	W	M		K	W	M		
1st November			1	1					Lieut I.m Metcalfe
3rd "						2		2	
10th "						1		1	
18th "		1		1	1			1	Lt C.L. de Hinds slightly at du...
19th "						1		1	
22nd "						1		1	
23rd "						1x		1	x Slightly at duty
26th "					1			1	
30th "	1			1					Lt W.h. Pruthell
TOTAL	2	1		3	2	6		8	

Dec 2nd 1917.

P.T.R...
LIEUT. CO...
COMMANDING 3rd WORCESTERSHIRE REG...

Army Form C. 2118.

3 Monters Ree RF

WAR DIARY
or
INTELLIGENCE SUMMARY.
(Erase heading not required.)

Instructions regarding War Diaries and Intelligence Summaries are contained in F. S. Regs., Part II. and the Staff Manual respectively. Title pages will be prepared in manuscript.

(Dec. 17 to May '18)

M39

Place	Date	Hour	Summary of Events and Information	Remarks and references to Appendices
CAMBRAI Sector	1917. Dec. 1.		Bn. in trenches. A Thurs raid planned by nature T.M. & Artillery bombardment, attacked against our line about 12.30 am. Enemy after some attacks entered at one unoccupied point 30. Withdrew & There left before day discovered.	Ref: Sheet 30.
	2.		Bn. relieved by 1/5" Leicestershire Regt. (46" Div.) & marched to LABEUVRIÈRE.	
	3.		Bn. at LABEUVRIÈRE.	
	4.		Bn. entrained at CHOCQUES, 4.30 p.m. for Third Army area.	
	5.		Bn. detrained at ACHIET-LE-GRAND, & marched to camp at ACHIET-LE-PETIT. Huts.	Ref: Sheet 57c.
	6.		Bn. marched to camp at FAVREUIL.	
LAGNICOURT S. Sector	7. to		Bn. marched up & relieved supports & C Coy. centre on line taken over a Sector of 145 front from 3rd Div. Bn. remained in till 16 inst. in reliefs & reliefs.	
	10.		Bn. moved back to wire AVAUX & BAUCOURT in the reserve.	
	c.			
	13th		Bn. took over trenches from 9" L.N. Lancs Regt. Sector extended from D20985 to D13 D 55.05. 11 hours Lewis Key, no myth ft 7 Le 15 no overlaps	
	19th		Bn. relieved by 9" L.N. Lancs Regt. & after an uneventful tour, my in 2h7 & cmp at BEUGNATRE. Except locally had neither entered Vigorous Patrols	back to reserve Vigorous Patrols

J. 37

WAR DIARY or INTELLIGENCE SUMMARY

Army Form C. 2118.

(Erase heading not required.)

Instructions regarding War Diaries and Intelligence Summaries are contained in F. S. Regs., Part II. and the Staff Manual respectively. Title pages will be prepared in manuscript.

Place	Date	Hour	Summary of Events and Information	Remarks and references to Appendices
LAGNICOURT S. Sector	1917 Dec.		under the same myself, but no trace of the enemy seen.	
	23.		Bn relieved 1st L.N. Lanc. in same sector as before.	
	25.		2/Lt A.B. FRYER & 2/Lt H. JONES went out at dusk to inspect wire belt (wire about 60 yds in front of our existing line) & did not return. A small patrol in the neighbourhood was heard to fire the shots but not afterwards failed to determine trace of either.	
	27.		A heavy shout at at 5 a.m. came under heavy M.G. fire, losing 2 killed & 8 seriously wounded. The wounded were brought in. 2/Lt SHAW, who was in command of the patrol & was behind wire, went out again & brought in the bodies of 2/Lt Killed, under great difficulties, in the bright moonlight, & saw Bn relieved in the afternoon by 9th L.N. Lancs. Regt., & marching the support, where having transferred to fighting Coys, which had previously been sent as escort.	
	31.		Bn relieved 9th L.N. Lancs Regt as before, Rest part extended throughout the month.	

Pronville, HCA
Capt 3/ Worcestershire Regt.

Casualties during December 1917

Date	Officers K	W	M	Total Officers	Other Ranks K	W	M	Total Other Ranks	Remarks
15-12-17	-	-	-	-	-	1	-	1	
17-12-17	-	1ˣ	-	1	1	-	-	1	ˣCaptain J.N. Little
25-12-17	-	-	2°	2	-	1	-	1	°Lieut. A.E. Fryer
26-12-17	-	-	-	-	-	1	-	1	" E.H. Jones
27-12-17	-	-	-	-	2	3	-	5	
Totals	-	1	2	3	3	6	-	9	

31st December 1917

P. Russell
LIEUT. COL.
COMMANDING 3rd WORCESTERSHIRE REGT.

WAR DIARY
or
INTELLIGENCE SUMMARY.

Army Form C. 2118.

2/7 3 Worcester Regt

Vol 41

J. 38

Place	Date	Hour	Summary of Events and Information	Remarks and references to Appendices
PRONVILLE SECTOR SHEET 57c I/40000	1918 Jan 1		A very cold tour; owing to great shortage of officers, own usual offensive patrolling could not be carried out. Enemy artillery were more active than usual, shelling the vicinity of Bn Hq with 4.2 and 5.9 on the 2nd and 3rd	
	4 to 8		The Bn was relieved by the 9th Royal Welsh Lancashire Regt and moved to Bde Reserve at Ussy Camp. Christmas Day was kept on the 5th; men had a good Christmas dinner of pork and plum pudding and beer.	
	8th		The Bn relieved the 9th Royal Welsh Lancashire Regt in the front line. Snow fell heavily all the morning and afternoon making it going very difficult.	
	9th		Thaw set in; trenches very muddy. Quiet tour; usual offensive patrolling	
	10th		The Bn relieved by 9th Royal North Lancashire Regt, & moved to Bde Support	

Army Form C. 2118.

WAR DIARY
or
INTELLIGENCE SUMMARY.
(Erase heading not required.)

Instructions regarding War Diaries and Intelligence Summaries are contained in F.S. Regs., Part II. and the Staff Manual respectively. Title pages will be prepared in manuscript.

Place	Date	Hour	Summary of Events and Information	Remarks and references to Appendices
	12th		Bn detailed to do special patrol work while in support A & C to told off for this, object being to capture a prisoner.	
			Two working cos. putting out wire every night on Bde left flank.	
	14th		Strong patrol of 2 officers & 25 o.r. of A Co with resistance from artillery attempted small enterprise against enemy wire, where our men were being out & some men infected.	
			Task untenable owing to being too thin. Close & irregular, resulting in no prisoner captured & 6 casualties to our men.	
NEST	15th & 16th		Rained for two days, all trenches falling in.	
321a.99 Sheet 57c.				
	17th		Relieved by 1st Loyal North Lancashire Regt on left sub-sector. Trenches impassable, all traffic had to go over the open.	
	18th		Hostile artillery more active probably due to increased movement in the open.	

A3834 Wt.W4973/M687 750,000 8/16 D.D. & L. Ltd. Forms/C.2118/13

WAR DIARY
or
INTELLIGENCE SUMMARY.
(Erase heading not required.)

Army Form C. 2118.

Place	Date	Hour	Summary of Events and Information	Remarks and references to Appendices
	22nd		Work during whole tour confined to clearing front line trench, which was impassable at the end of tour. Usual patrols sent out. Relieved by part of 1st Loyal N. Lancashire Regt who took over whole 1 Bde Front. Dispositions changed to 1 Bn in front line. 1 Bn in Support one. Bn in reserve + 1 Bn on works only. Bn moved into Reserve dtts No 7 Camp.	
	22nd to 26th		Bn at No 7 Camp resting & cleaning up.	
	26th		Bn relieved 1st Loyal N Lancs Regt on whole Bde front. Bn Boundaries now. Left D20a 2.6 Right D21d.9.4 (Sheet 57d)	
	to		Quiet tour.	
	31st		Bn relieved by 1st Loyal North Lancashire Regt & became Bn in Bde Support.	

R.J. Price
Major
COMMANDING 3rd WORCESTERSHIRE

3RD BN. The Worcestershire Regiment
Casualties during January 1918.

Date	Officers			Total	Other Ranks			Total
	K	W	M		K	W	M	
1st						2		2
3rd					1	2		3
4th						1		1
9th						2		2
13th						1		1
14th						5	1	6
15th						1		1
16th						1		1
18th						1		1
19th						1		1
								19

2nd February 1918

R.F. Trice, Major
COMMANDING 3rd WORCESTERSHIRE REGT.

WAR DIARY or INTELLIGENCE SUMMARY

Army Form C. 2118.

3rd Bn Worcester Regt

Y.39

Place	Date	Hour	Summary of Events and Information	Remarks and references to Appendices
	1st Feb to 5th		Bn in Bde Support. 2 Companies wiring every night + 2 companies working on Support Trenches. 13th Cheshire Regt disbanded, now only 3 Bns in the Bde. Bn relieved part of 9th Loyal N. Lancs Regt in left sub sector. Quiet tour except fatalities accident.	
	6th 8th		Bn relieved by part of 11th Lancashire Fusiliers who took over whole Bde front.	
	9th to 11th		Bn in Bde Reserve, washing + cleaning up.	
	11th to 22nd		Relief of Divison by 6th Division. Bn marched to ACHIET AREA. Bn rebilleted in huts. (BUCHANNAN CAMP.) Bn in Training at BUCHANNAN CAMP. A good deal of musketry done on ACHIET-LE-PETIT ranges & about range. Two drafts of 13 & 97 joined Bn from Royal Worcesters & West Yorks, all under 20 years of age. Casualties for Month Nil	FRANKLEY Lt Col Cmd 3/Worcester Regt

25th Division.
74th Infantry Brigade.

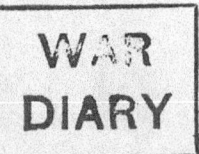

3rd BATTALION

THE WORCESTER REGIMENT

MARCH 1918

Army Form C. 2118.

WAR DIARY or INTELLIGENCE SUMMARY.

3rd Bn Newcastle Regt

(Erase heading not required.)

Place	Date	Hour	Summary of Events and Information	Remarks and references to Appendices
ACHIET	March 1st to 11th		Bn in training. Bn musketry classification fired. Bn average 78 as against 48 & 49 of the other 2 Bns in the Bde.	
	12th		Bn moved to No 11 Camp FAVREUIL, in rehearsal for expected German offensive, remaining here until 21st inst, engaged training, further working parties.	
	21st	5 am	Heavy German bombardment of front system & back areas commenced. A few shells fell near camp, doing no damage. Bn had breakfasts & prepared to move.	
		5.15am		
		10 noon	Orders received to move to FREMICOURT. Bn on arrival at FREMICOURT Bn ordered to take up a position astride the BAPAUME & CAMBRAI Rd. 1000 yds west of BEUGNY.	
Map 57 C.		6.15pm	Orders to afford breach of Corps Line about VAULX WOOD. Bn were ordered to put one company into the Corps Line East of MORCHIES with 2 Coys to form a defensive flank from northern end of MORCHIES to MARICOURT WOOD. One company was ordered to remain in reserve with Bn HQ in Sunken Road I.S.C. On arrival at Corps Line, it was found to be full of troops of 6th Division, no coy. move disposed on night 21st/22nd.	

Army Form C. 2118.

WAR DIARY
or
INTELLIGENCE SUMMARY.
(Erase heading not required.)

Place	Date	Hour	Summary of Events and Information	Remarks and references to Appendices
Map 57 C.			as follows:	
			A Co (Co Comdr. Lt F.G. Elliott until killed in action 22.3.18, then 2 Lt W.B. Parker, Lt 6th subsequently 2 Lt E.W. Prickles) dug in on line I5a 5.7 to I5a 5.0.	
			B Co (Co Comdr. Capt J.M. Lett until killed in action 22.3.18, then Capt E. Letty) dug in along sunken rd from I4d 6.7 to I5c 3.8.	
			D Co (Co Comdr. 2 Lt W.V. Short) dug in along sunken road from I5c 4.8 to I5d 4.4.	
			C Co (Co Comdr. Capt E.V.R. Parsons) dug in from T10 & 9.6 to I10b 6.1.	
	22nd	9 am	Bn H.Q. moved to deep dug out at I17a.	
		7.45 am	Major F.T. Small took over command of Bn that a.m. R.W. Wyffe Esq. city was ordered fwd to R.W.C.R. B & C Cos were ordered to extend left flank along northern	
		10 am	side of MARICOURT WOOD & towards VAULX WOOD where fresh attacks were taking place on the CORPS LINE.	
		4.50 pm	Owing to withdrawal of a Bn on the left B & C Coys were ordered to withdraw to sunken road in I17a. Owing to fresh enemy attacks developing only C Co could be extricated. In the meantime	

WAR DIARY or INTELLIGENCE SUMMARY.

Army Form C. 2118.

(Erase heading not required.)

Place	Date	Hour	Summary of Events and Information	Remarks and references to Appendices
			A & B Coys had some stiff fighting, inflicting heavy casualties on the enemy.	
		7 pm	Situation on the left became serious & Bn was ordered to form a defensive flank between BEETROOT FACTORY & I.17.a. B Coy could not be extricated from its position but C.Q.D. Coy with elements of 51st Division held a position between I.17.a central and BEETROOT FACTORY, while A Coy held a position north of the Sunken Rd near Bn HQ in I.17.a.	
Mch 5/17			During the day the following officers became casualties. Capt J.M. Rott killed, Lt A.D. McMunn killed, Lt F.J. Elliott killed. 2 Lt A. Houghton killed, 2 Lt C. Clatham wounded. Bn was withdrawn to FREMICOURT.	
	23rd	3 am	Bn was ordered to march to BIHUCOURT CHURCH when 74th Inf Bde was concentrating. Bn remained in SAVOY CAMP BIHUCOURT that night & until 3 pm 24th.	
		1.45 pm		
	24th	3 pm	Bn was ordered to dig in on line C.2.d.70.15 to C.29.a.02.80.	
	25th	1 am	During the troops on left flank withdrawing Bn withdrew & took over	

WAR DIARY
or
INTELLIGENCE SUMMARY.
(Erase heading not required.)

Army Form C. 2118.

Place	Date	Hour	Summary of Events and Information	Remarks and references to Appendices
		2.10 p.m	a position on the night - 11th Lancashire Fusiliers on Ridge G.23.a with 9th Royal North Lancs on the left - 11th Lancashire Fusiliers on the flanks being refused B/n took up position in G.21.a + b. where it was fired on by our own artillery and where it was fired on by our own artillery By this time troops were streaming back on the right of the B/n together with 11th Lancashire Fusiliers moved to the west of the railway, owing again to insecurity of flanks.	Reference Map 57 c.
		3.30 p.m	An enemy tried to push on the B/n again crossed to Railway + held a line along old communication trench from I.20.d to I.15.c.35.45.	
		6 p.m	Owing to withdrawal of 41st Division on the right the B/n recrossed the railway + held old German trenches from I.14.d central to I.15.b.7.1. From this line the B/de was withdrawn through 62nd Division who were dug in east of ACHIET-LE-PETIT + assembled at BUCQUOY. B/n spent the night	Ref Sheet 57 d.

Army Form C. 2118.

WAR DIARY
or
INTELLIGENCE SUMMARY.
(Erase heading not required.)

Instructions regarding War Diaries and Intelligence Summaries are contained in F. S. Regs., Part II. and the Staff Manual respectively. Title pages will be prepared in manuscript.

Place	Date	Hour	Summary of Events and Information	Remarks and references to Appendices
at BATTEMOY FM.	26th	9.15 am	Orders received to move to F14a central, where Bn awaited further orders.	Ref Sheet 57 d.
		12 noon	Orders received verbally for Bn to take up position with right at E29 L 00.80 & right on LA BRAYELLE Fm. Bn in position by 5pm.	
		5 pm	Orders received to side-step to the left in order to make room for the 7d Bde who were coming in on the night. Bn night now on LA BRAYELLE FM.	
		11.30pm	Warning order received that Bn was to withdraw to Bde assembly point west of FONQUEVILLERS or SOUASTRE road.	
	27th		Bn arrived at assembly point about 2.15 am, where orders were received to march to COUIN, 8 miles, where the whole Bde were concentrated by 7.30 am.	
		2.30pm	Bn Marched to PUCHVILLERS, 10 miles, where it spent the	

Army Form C. 2118.

WAR DIARY
or
INTELLIGENCE SUMMARY.
(Erase heading not required.)

Instructions regarding War Diaries and Intelligence Summaries are contained in F. S. Regs., Part II. and the Staff Manual respectively. Title pages will be prepared in manuscript.

Place	Date	Hour	Summary of Events and Information	Remarks and references to Appendices
ST OUEN	28th	8am	The night in the open. after very cold night, Bn marched to billets in ST OUEN 14 miles. Men marched very well covering nearly 36 miles in 36 hours.	
	29th 30th		Bn resting	
	31st	8 am	Bn marched to CANDAS. 10 miles, preparatory to entraining for Second Army area.	
		4 pm	Bn entrained	

Prewle........... LIEUT. COL.
COMMANDING 3rd WORCESTERSHIRE REGT.

CASUALTIES in 3RD BN. THE WORCESTERSHIRE REGIMENT DURING MARCH 1918

DATES	OFFICERS			TOTAL OFFICER CASUALTIES	OTHER RANKS			TOTAL OTHER RANKS CASUALTIES	REMARKS
	K	W	M		K	W	M		
Noon 21/3/18 to Noon 22/3/18	3	1	-	4	14	49	-	63	Includes 27 Wounded and 10 Wounded at duty
22/3/18 — 23/3/18	1	-	-	1	2	49	-	51	
23/3/18 — 24/3/18	-	-	-	-	1	-	-	1	
24/3/18 — 25/3/18	-	-	-	-	-	1	30	31	
25/3/18 —	-	-	-	5	30	-	-	162	

P.C. Mullan .... LIEUT. COL.
COMMANDING 3rd WORCESTERSHIRE REGT.

25th Division.
74th Infantry Brigade.

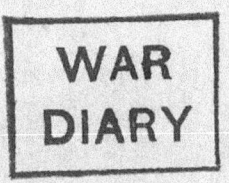

3rd BATTALION

THE WORCESTERSHIRE REGIMENT

APRIL 1918

WAR DIARY
INTELLIGENCE SUMMARY
(Erase heading not required.)

Army Form C. 2118.

2nd Worcesters

Place	Date	Hour	Summary of Events and Information	Remarks and references to Appendices
CAESTRE	April 1st	9.30am	Bn detrained and moved by Lorry route to ALDERSHOT CAMP near NEUVE EGLISE.	MinBrown(?)
	2nd		Bn relieved 27th Bn A.I.F. in de LE TOUQUET sector.	
	2nd		Bn in trenches. Q met tour and no casualties.	
	3rd			
	4th			
	5th		Bn relieved by 8th Border Regt. & moved to ALDERSHOT CAMP.	
	6th		Bn resting & refitting at ALDERSHOT CAMP.	
	7th			
	8th			
	9th	4pm	Battle of the LYS began.	L.40
		12.45pm	Bn ordered to move at once to concentration area at STEENWERCK.	
		3.45pm	Bn ordered to move to position on north bank of LYS river with right at H2c.1.9.	Ref Map Sheet 36 1/40000
		4.30pm	Bn moved off, and front line under Machine Gun fire at L'HALLOBEAU. Few casualties owing to fire being high.	
			Bn got into position about 6pm with A B & C Co in front line &	

Army Form C. 2118.

WAR DIARY
or
INTELLIGENCE SUMMARY.
(Erase heading not required.)

Place	Date	Hour	Summary of Events and Information	Remarks and references to Appendices
	9th		9 D Co in reserve. Elements of 34th Divison went in front of us on our left. Failed to get in touch on the right owing to 11th Lancashire Fusiliers being held up at CROIX DU BAC.	Reference Map Sheet 36. 1/40,000.
		6.30p	D Co sent to support 11th Lancashire Fusiliers who were attacking CROIX DU BAC.	
	10th	2am	In conjunction with 11th Lanc: Fus: who were attacking CROIX DU BAC Bn made good BERKSHIRE, SUSSEX & LANCASHIRE Posts.	
		10.30am	During the night 2 prisoners were captured. Right flank had to be drawn back from BERKSHIRE & SUSSEX POSTS owing to enemy working his way round right flank. Owing to enemy advancing in force round right flank Bn had to withdraw & took up new position with left on L'HALLOBEAU. Flank this position severe casualties were inflicted on the enemy by Lewis gun & rifle fire.	
		2.30p	The Bn again had to withdraw & took up position on the STEENWERCK – ARMENTIERES railway, with right on	

WAR DIARY
or
INTELLIGENCE SUMMARY.

(Erase heading not required.)

Army Form C. 2118.

Place	Date	Hour	Summary of Events and Information	Remarks and references to Appendices
STEENWERCK Station.	10th	6 pm	Enemy came along railway from TROIS ARBRES and attacked our left flank, capturing Lt.H.V.RICHARDS, the Bn Lewis gun officer. The position now became untenable owing to Enfilade M.G. fire & Bn withdrew about 300x & took up touch with position on right of 88th Bde, & got in touch with 4 Worcestershire Regt. Bn. now in support to 74 Bde. Following officer casualties recurred during the day :- Capt F.A.Reading M.C. Capt. A.Bower M.C. Lt.A.V.P.Rowland, Lt.Curt, & 2 Lt. A.B. Rowe wounded. During night the pressure had ceased and the Machine gun fire had become less.	
	11th	8.20 am	Bn advanced to attack STEENWERCK. Very heavy machine gun fire was encountered & owing to both flanks of the Bde being attached the Bn had to withdraw	
		2 pm	to line of light railway astride the ST LBECQUE Bn held this line for remainder of the day.	

WAR DIARY
or
INTELLIGENCE SUMMARY.

(Erase heading not required.)

Army Form C. 2118.

Place	Date	Hour	Summary of Events and Information	Remarks and references to Appendices
	12d		Bn. held line of Railway throughout the day, dispersing enemy patrols by Lewis gun & rifle fire.	
	13d	9.30am	Precautionary order received from Bde. to the effect that in case of withdrawal Bde. would retire now at MONT DE LILLE S22c.00.00.	Ref. Map 28/40,000
		12mn.	Bn. began evacuating position, owing to critical situation on the flanks, & commenced march to MONT DE LILLE.	
	16d	5am	Bn. commenced digging in on MONT DE LILLE. Enemy lost no time in following up withdrawal and at 7.30am a strong enemy patrol dressed in British uniform approached 20 men of the 4th W. Yorkshire Regt who were still on our immediate left.	
		9.30am	Heavy bombardment opened on our front line & supports. Enemy advanced to the attack but were driven off by Lewis gun & rifle fire.	
		11.55am	Very heavy bombardment continued throughout the day causing about 50 casualties in the Bn., 2 Lt. J.A. Bourke being killed & Lt. R.R. Giles wounded.	

WAR DIARY or INTELLIGENCE SUMMARY

Army Form C. 2118.

Place	Date	Hour	Summary of Events and Information	Remarks and references to Appendices
	14th	8pm	Party of about 50 of the enemy advanced towards our line at the foot of MONT DELILLE. In conjunction with the Bn on our flanks, they were driven back, the Bn capturing 4 prisoners & 2 Machine guns and killing about 30 of the enemy. The line was thus restored to its original position.	Ref. Map Sheet 28 1/20,000
	15th	4.30am	The Bn was relieved by a Bn. of the N. Staff. (59th Division) & proceeded to B de Nenday - from S.2.d.2.7. where hot breakfasts were served. During the day Bn dug in on line between S3.C. 76.75 to S.3.d. 9.5.65. Owing to enemy attacking & breaking through 59th Division lines Bn again found itself in front line.	
	16th	7pm	Bn still in same position. Quiet day on the whole except for slight shelling of front line. 2 Lt P.H.C. Constable being wounded.	
	17th	10.30am	Heavy shelling of front line & back areas commenced & went on intermittently all day.	

Army Form C. 2118.

WAR DIARY
or
INTELLIGENCE SUMMARY.
(Erase heading not required.)

Instructions regarding War Diaries and Intelligence Summaries are contained in F. S. Regs., Part II. and the Staff Manual respectively. Title pages will be prepared in manuscript.

Place	Date	Hour	Summary of Events and Information	Remarks and references to Appendices
	17th / 18th		During the night 17/18th Bn was relieved by a Bn of 102 Bde. On relief Bn moved into close support to 6th Duke of Wellingtons 147th Bde.	
	19th		Bn dug in at M31 d.8.5. Quiet day except for a few shells round D co, which caused 4 casualties.	
	20th		Another quiet day.	
	21st	4am	Bn evacuated Spoonbill position, as 34th Division (to which 7th Bde had been attached throughout the operations) was relieved by 133rd French Division. Bn marched to HOOGRAAF CABARET, where hot breakfasts were served.	
		12.30pm	Bn marched to DIRTY BUCKET area, where the Bde rejoined 25th Division.	
	22nd to 25th		Bn training & refitting in BRAKE CAMP. Reinforcements of 13 officers & 250 other ranks joined Bn.	
	25th	12.15pm	Orders received that Division were under an hour's notice to move in close support of XXII Corps.	
		12.30pm	Orders received to move at 1.30 pm.	

Army Form C. 2118.

WAR DIARY
or
INTELLIGENCE SUMMARY.
(Erase heading not required.)

Instructions regarding War Diaries and Intelligence Summaries are contained in F. S. Regs., Part II. and the Staff Manual respectively. Title pages will be prepared in manuscript.

Place	Date	Hour	Summary of Events and Information	Remarks and references to Appendices
	25	1.30pm	Bn moved & reached place of assembly 27 C.o.S nr MOOGRAAF CABT. at 6.30pm.	Reference: Map 28 1/20000
		7pm.	Two patrols sent out under 2Lt W.H. Parker M.C. & Lt J.R. Duffield to reconnoitre route to LACLYTTE & to report on position of our troops (if any) also position of enemy. Patrols both brought back most useful information. Capt E.O. Tindall now took command of Bn. Team.	
		8.30pm	Orders received to move to vicinity of LACLYTTE & await orders.	
	26th	1.30am	Orders received that the Bn would counter-attack the next morning in the vicinity direction of KEMMEL village.	
		3am	Bn commenced counter attack with A + D in front C Co in support B Co in reserve. Barrage very poor, country very difficult. First objective taken with practically no casualties. Leading companies reached second objective (KEMMEL village) but right flank held up, owing to 9th Inf Bde not advancing to 9th Inf Bde came up on our left, but fell back, without	

WAR DIARY
or
INTELLIGENCE SUMMARY.
(Erase heading not required.)

Army Form C. 2118.

Place	Date	Hour	Summary of Events and Information	Remarks and references to Appendices
			our knowledge, leaving our left flank in the air. Enemy then entered Byron to its own machine-gun fire from both flanks. The position was untenable & under cover of the mist the Bde was withdrawn to the line of railway behind KEMMELBEKE Stream where it intended to reorganize & dig in. During the counter-attack the following officers became Casualties. 2 Lt A Chigwell (killed), 2 Lt W. H. Hartley M.C. (killed), Capt E.V.P. Paxon (wounded & missing), Capt M. Andrewman (wounded), 2 Lt A.L.S. Savory (wounded), 2 Lt L.B. Whittingham (wounded, died later), 2 Lt B.J. Mason (wounded). Bn held line of railway during the day. Shelling very heavy, especially during the afternoon.	
	27th		Bn still holding line of railway. Shelling still heavy. Ref. Map Night of 27th/28th Bn relieved by 8th Border Regt 75th Inf Bde 28/1/29 000 & moved to H31.C. Bn in 2nd Divisional Support.	
	28th		Bn heavily shelled. Lt Bonney 2Lt A.E. Brougain being killed & 2Lt I.N Fothergill wounded.	

WAR DIARY or INTELLIGENCE SUMMARY.

Army Form C. 2118.

Place	Date	Hour	Summary of Events and Information	Remarks and references to Appendices
	29th	2p	Enemy attacked all along the line, but repulsed at every point along Divisional front. Enemy unconfirmed message received that a mass on MONT ROUGE MONT VIDAIGNE & SCHERPENBERG, and Bn was ordered to dig defensive flank in M.12.b. D. It was found that the situation reconnoitring position was normal & that enemy were not in possession of any of the above mentioned heights. Bde were immediately informed of this & Bn was withdrawn to H.31.C where they remained for the rest of the day.	Ref. Map Sheet 28 1/40,000
	30th		Night 29th/30th Bn relieved 4th K.O.Y.L.I. 148th Bde in the front line. Heavily shelled with gas & H.E. before & during the day. Bn suffered continuously & shelled intermittently during the day.	

R. Price
Major.
COMMANDING 3rd WORCESTERSHIRE REGT.

3rd Bn The Worcestershire Regt

Casualties during April

Date	Officers			Total	O. Ranks			Total O.R.	
	K	W	M		K	W	M		
Noon 9th to Noon 10th	-	6	-	6	18	93	51	162	x 9 B.P. / 1 D & 16 / A.M. & 17 / 2 AS & 17
" 10 " 11	-	-	-	-	7	52	12	71	x 1 D.W. 16 / Ø 1 B.P.
" 11 " 12	-	-	-	-	2	24	1	25	x 1 D.W.
" 12 " 13	1	-	-	1	1	3	-	4	
" 13 " 14	2	1	-	3	3	9	1	13	
" 14 " 15	-	-	-	-	-	1	-	1	
" 15 " 16	-	1	-	1	-	13	1	14	
" 16 " 17	-	-	-	-	2	7	1	10	
" 17 " 18	-	-	-	-	1	2	-	3	
" 18 " 19	-	-	-	-	-	2	-	2	
" 19 " 20	-	-	-	-	1	4	-	5	
" 25 " 26	2	4	-	6	9	63	10	82	Ø 1 B.P. / 1 D.W. / = 1 B.P.
" 26 " 27	6	2	-	8	2	5	1	8	
" 27 " 28	-	-	-	-	1	13	-	14	
" 28 " 29	-	-	-	-	1	15	2	18	
" 29 " 30	-	-	-	-	2	2	-	4	
				25				436	

1st May 1915

Major
Commanding 3rd Worcestershire Regt.

to 57/19 4 Jun.

3 Worcester Regt

Vol 45

WAR DIARY
or
INTELLIGENCE SUMMARY.
(Erase heading not required.)

Army Form C. 2118.

Place	Date	Hour	Summary of Events and Information	Remarks and references to Appendices
	May 1st		Bn still in front line.	
	2nd		Bn relieved on night 1st/2nd by 1/4 York & Lancaster, & moved to 6.27.B. C.2.I.C. Bn were under orders of G.O.C. 49th Division & under 2 hours notice to move.	
	3rd	9 pm	Bn moved to L.23.b. Still under 49th Division	Ref. Map Sheet 27 1/40,000
	4th	4 pm	Bn moved to ST ELOI CART. where it rejoined 25th Division	Ditto
	5th	10 am	Spent the day resting.	
	5th to 8th		Bn moved to LA BELLE VUE area near WORMHOUDT. Bn resting & reorganizing near WORMHOUDT.	Ref. Map HAZEBROUCK 5A 1/100,000
	9th	2.45 am	Bn entrained at WAYENBERG for IX Corps area (6th French Army)	Ref. Map SOISSONS 22 1/100,000
	11	12 noon	Bn detrained at FÈRE-EN-TARDENOIS, & marched to camp at COULANGES.	
	11th to 22nd		Bn in training & refitting at COULANGES. Very hot weather experienced during this period.	" "
	23rd	7.30 p	Bn marched to camp & billets in VANDEVIL.	

Army Form C. 2118.

WAR DIARY
or
INTELLIGENCE SUMMARY.
(Erase heading not required.)

Place	Date	Hour	Summary of Events and Information	Remarks and references to Appendices
	22nd to 26th		Bn in training at VANDEUIL.	Reference Map SOISSONS. 1/40,000
	26th	7.30 pm	Warning order received that Bn was to be ready to move to MUSCOURT at 8 pm.	
		10 pm	Orders received to move to MUSCOURT, owing to expected German attack at dawn	
	27th	1 am	Bombardment began.	
		8 am	Bn arrived at MUSCOURT.	
		8.30 am	Bn was put at disposal of 50th Division	
		4.15 am	Bn moved up to CONCEVREUX, & took at pontoon with A & B Companies covering the bridgehead at CONCEVREUX. C Company formed a defensive flank almost at right angles to the Canal (The enemy had crossed the Canal at PONTAVERT & were moving in a South Westerly direction) and D Company were in reserve in trenches on slopes south of CONCEVREUX.	

WAR DIARY
or
INTELLIGENCE SUMMARY.
(Erase heading not required.)

Army Form C. 2118.

Place	Date	Hour	Summary of Events and Information	Remarks and references to Appendices
	27th	2.30pm	Enemy broke through Bn. on our right & worked behind the three front line companies & got into CONCEVREUX. After heavy casualties the Bn. managed to withdraw & take up position on high ground south of CONCEVREUX with left of position on CONCEVREUX - VENTELAY road. Bn. now about 120 strong. In the fighting around CONCEVREUX Bn. now further got separated & withdrew too far to the left.	Ref map SOISSONS 1/40,000.
		10.30pm	Bn. again had to withdraw to SW of VENTELAY. Following officer casualties occurred during the day: Capt E.A. Humphries MC (missing) 2Lt E.V. Mathews (missing) 2Lt R.O. Godden (wounded & missing) Lt W.B.J Wall (wounded & missing) Capt T. Grant (wounded)	
	28th	7am	Bn. ordered to withdraw to LES VENTEAUX - MONTIGNY road. Bn. now holding high ground N.W of MONTIGNY. The enemy now holding ground South of BOUVANCOURT, it was there decided to withdraw. Bn. was now very badly situated.	
		1pm	Stragglers found their way to transport lines at LAGERY & efforts were made to reorganise what was left of Bn. into one Company.	

WAR DIARY
or
INTELLIGENCE SUMMARY.
(Erase heading not required.)

Army Form C. 2118.

Place	Date	Hour	Summary of Events and Information	Remarks and references to Appendices
	28th	9pm	Enemy reported to be in possession of CRUGNY so Transport & remnants of Bn moved to AOUGNY where they spent the night. Following officer casualties occurred during the day, Lt J.T. Milner (wounded), 2Lt V.B. Wooley (missing) Capt T.P. Mugglethwaite who was with composite Bn composed of 3 Teams & Bde I.M. trench mortar platoon	
	29th	7am	Remnants of Bn & Transport moved to PASSY where it was thought that Bn touch might be obtained with 74d Bde	
		8pm	Bn was ordered by Divn to move to ROMIGNY, where 74d Bde HQ was found to be.	
		8pm	Bn lay on line of TRAMERY – LHERY Road in support of 19d Divn.	
	30th	10.30am	During & troops of ds left falling back Bn withdrew to BARNE SARCY – VILLE EN TARDENOIS in touch with ds Loyal N. Lancs Regt on ds right & 10d Worcestershire Regt on ds night	
		12 noon	Bn now holding ground S.W of VILLE-EN-TARDENOIS which was held for ds remainder of ds day.	

Army Form C. 2118.

WAR DIARY
or
INTELLIGENCE SUMMARY.
(Erase heading not required.)

Place	Date	Hour	Summary of Events and Information	Remarks and references to Appendices
	31st		Bn in same position all day.	

R. Norie Major
COMMANDING 3rd WORCESTERSHIRE REGT.

In line 5 the second "right" should read "left"

25/4/27

www.ingramcontent.com/pod-product-compliance
Lightning Source LLC
Chambersburg PA
CBHW082013220426
43670CB00014B/2612